SAINTS

SAINTS

SEVENTY STORIES OF FAITH

ALEXANDRA BONFANTE-WARREN

COURAGE BOOKS

AN IMPRINT OF RUNNING PRESS
PHILADELPHIA · LONDON

©2000 by Michael Friedman Publishing Group, Inc.

First published in the United States in 2000 by Courage Books.

Printed in China

10 9 8 7 6 5 4 3 2 1

Digit on the right indicates the number of this printing.

Library of Congress Cataloging-in-Publication Number 99-74358

ISBN 0-7624-0684-4

Saints
was prepared and produced by
Michael Friedman Publishing Group, Inc.
15 West 26th Street
New York, New York 10010

Editor: Celeste Sollod
Art Director: Jeff Batzli
Designer: Amanda Wilson
Photography Editor: Valerie E. Kennedy
Production Manager: Camille Lee

This book may be ordered by mail from the publisher. *But try your bookstore first!*

Published by Courage Books, an imprint of
Running Press Book Publishers
125 South Twenty-second Street
Philadelphia, Pennsylvania 19103-4399

Visit us on the web!
www.runningpress.com

FRONTISPIECE: *This elaborate panel, painted in 1674 by Master Radoule for the Church of the Patriarchy in Kosovo Polje, in the former Yugoslavia, shows the beloved twin brothers and physicians Cosmas and Damian, surrounded by scenes of their wonders.*

Dedication

For Suor Maria Teresa Cuneo

*The arc of Christ's life on earth is illustrated in this fourteenth-century
Italian triptych, or three-part altarpiece, by Andrea di Firenze.*

Contents

DAVID

JACOB PRIARCA

ESAIAS

SIMILIS FACTV VM PELLICANO SOLITVDINIS

IESVS NAZARENVS·REX·IVDEORVM

IN SITI MEA POTAVERVT ME ACETO

ADIREDAH DESCENDISTI FILI MI LEO
DORMIENS ACCVBVISTI VT LEO

SVM

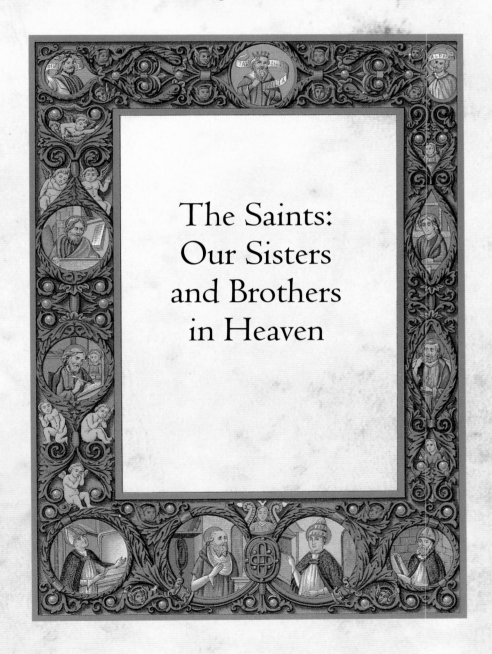

The Saints:
Our Sisters
and Brothers
in Heaven

FOR THOUSANDS OF YEARS, SAINTS HAVE HELD GREAT POWER OVER OUR IMAGINATIONS, REGARDLESS OF OUR PERSONAL RELIGIOUS FEELINGS—OR LACK OF THEM. IN THE NEW TESTAMENT, THE COMMUNITY OF CHRISTIANS CONSECRATED TO GOD THROUGH THE SACRAMENT OF BAPTISM ARE CALLED "SAINTS"—THIS IS THE TERM BY WHICH SAINT PAUL (P. 25), FOR EXAMPLE, ADDRESSES THE MEMBERS OF VARIOUS CHRISTIAN COMMUNITIES. THE RITUAL OF BAPTISM BRINGS THE CHRISTIAN INTO COMMUNION WITH CHRIST, AND DEDICATES THE CHRISTIAN TO GOD'S SERVICE, BUT THERE IS A PERSONAL MORAL EFFORT REQUIRED AS WELL IF THE CHRISTIAN IS TO WALK WITH GOD. THIS DESIRE FOR PERSONAL GOODNESS IS POSSIBLE BECAUSE HOLINESS REQUIRES FREE WILL AS MUCH AS DIVINE GRACE.

IN ROMAN CATHOLIC THEOLOGY, ALL HOLY ACTIONS ARE SUCH BECAUSE THEY ARE MOVED BY RELIGION, THAT IS, BECAUSE THEY ARE DONE IN THE SERVICE OF GOD. AS SUBMISSION TO GOD BECOMES PERFECTED, SOME PEOPLE ACHIEVE THE CHRISTLIKE EXERCISE OF VIRTUE: "FAITHFUL, CONSTANT, READY, TO THE POINT OF HEROISM." IT IS THIS STATE, MORE THAN ANY MIRACLES OR MYSTICISM, THAT THE CHURCH CONSIDERS "SAINTLY."

MARTYRS

In the first years of Christianity, the faithful looked to the martyrs as examples—after all, they were believers who had made the ultimate sacrifice for their faith. Rather than mourning them, the survivors felt joy that their comrades had gone to heaven, where they would see and be one with God. The saint's death day was considered a birthday, and was observed as a feast day, a day of celebration; likewise, the saint's tomb was an object of veneration and pilgrimage, the scene of miracles and prayers for intercession, that is, for the saint in heaven to turn Christ's benevolence toward a certain end. (In time, Catholic theology would see saints as physical extensions of Christ in the material world.)

The first martyred Christians after Christ himself, those of his generation, were put to death for political reasons, usually because they affirmed loyalty to a higher power than the secular authorities, no matter how exalted. Many of the saints in this collection were martyred during the wholesale persecutions pursued by the Roman emperors Diocletian (c. 245–316; emperor 284–305) and Maximian (emperor 286–305, 306–308; died 310), along with their fellow rulers, or caesars, Galerius (caesar 293–305; emperor 305–311; died 311) and Constantius Chlorus (caesar 293–305; emperor 305–306; died 306), husband of Saint Helena (p. 80) and father of Constantine, who made Christianity the favored religion of the Roman Empire.

PAGES 8 AND 9: Born Guido di Pietro, this Dominican painter-monk became known as "Beato Angelico," so heavenly were his works. A number of saints, mainly prelates and friars, here attend the Crucifixion.

RIGHT: From a fifteenth-century Book of Hours, this splendid miniature of the joyous community of the saints surely lifted readers' hearts to heaven.

ASCETICS

The anti-Christian measures of Diocletian and later of Julian, called the Apostate, were sometimes exercised against women who were dedicated virgins. Asceticism, or turning away from "the world" toward the Kingdom of God as shown by the virgins, would remain a characteristic of Catholicism, both Eastern and Western. Many religious persons went further than renouncing the goods and pleasures of the material world and actively engaged in "mortifications of the flesh," the active punishment of their bodies, in order to subdue distracting human impulses. Today, however, the Church discourages such practices in favor of a path of humble moderation.

THE CONFESSORS

The martyrs gave clear examples of heroic virtue, but after the periods of persecution, ordinary Christians also looked to those who exercised faith, hope, and charity at a higher level than most, and were consistently driven by their love of God and their neighbor in their daily lives. These holy people were spontaneously acknowledged as transcendently good by those about them—much as today we might describe someone as a "saint" who overcomes or endures a difficult situation with patience, inner strength, and grace. These splendid examples of Christian practice were the "confessors of the faith," or simply the "confessors."

The confessors were venerated like the martyrs, with special reverence being accorded their bodies, or relics; miracles, often of healing, were reported during their lifetimes or after their deaths. (A saint does not herself or himself perform miracles but rather, as a human being in communion with Christ, intercedes on behalf of those on earth.)

SAINTS' CULTS

Popular cults, centered on veneration of particular martyrs or confessors, grew. The local bishop approved the popular cult, and the saint's body was moved to the altar of a church.

Medieval Europe was a rigidly structured society, reflecting what was believed to be God's eternal and universal order, and each segment of this highly compartmentalized world was benevolently overseen by one or more patron saints. Thus, Catherine of Alexandria (page 51) and Thomas Aquinas were patrons of philosophers, Zita (page 94) of domestic servants, Nicholas (page 122) of sailors. In modern times, Catherine of Siena (page 64) is the patron saint of office workers, Fiacre of cab drivers.

OPPOSITE: Born a century after Saint Francis, the painter Simone Martini depicted the saint's stigmata—miraculous wounds like those of the crucified Christ—on his raised right hand and under his torn habit.

RIGHT: This French manuscript is one of countless editions of The Golden Legend, *a fourteenth-century anthology of miracles and other wonders.*

Daily life in the Middle Ages was organized by the church calendar—still today, in some cultures, people celebrate their name day, that is, their saint's day, rather than, or in addition to, their birthday.

There had been popes in Rome almost uninterruptedly since Peter, but in the highly decentralized Europe of the Middle Ages, the local bishops were the effective authority over their dioceses. As popular cults of saints multiplied, so did requests on the part of the faithful for more information on their chosen protectors. There sprang up a literature of saints' "legends." These texts were read as part of the Liturgy, the text of the Mass, and a number of biographies of the saints were written to provide examples of holiness.

The most famous of these compilations is *The Golden Legend*, written in the late thirteenth century. (A number of quotes in this book are taken from this collection of the Blessed Jacobus de Voragine's lively tales.) In church, the faithful could look about and recognize the saints pictured around them by their attributes, named in the legends: Barbara (page 50), shut up in a tower, carries a tower; Matilda (page 122), a queen, wears a crown; Lawrence (page 40) is shown with a grill. After following these inspiring accounts of spiritual power and ingenuity, the listeners returned, fortified, to the less dramatic but equally challenging trials of daily life.

CANONIZATION

The first recorded declaration of sainthood by the Holy See was that of Saint Uldaricus, in 973. Since then, the names of saints have been entered into a list, or "canon," and the saint is thereby said to be "canonized." The popes of the eleventh and twelfth centuries traveled more than their predecessors, and so themselves presided over the approval of cults, rather than the local bishops. In 1234, Pope Gregory IX made canonization an exclusive papal prerogative, though "equivalent" canonization, that is, approval following investigation by the Holy See of a popular cult that has endured more than one hundred years, continues to this day.

Since 1588, the Sacred Congregation of Rites has been the papal office that investigates the lives of those proposed for canonization. The Congregation ascertains whether the servant of God exhibited heroic virtue, or, in cases of possible martyrdom, whether death occurred *in odium fidei* ("because of hatred for the faith"). The writings of the person under consideration are examined for doctrinal purity, and at least two miracles attributed to the intercession of the candidate are investigated. There also exists a historical section of the Congregation of Rites, charged with, among other responsibilities, reviewing cases presented for equivalent canonization.

The pope, after hearing all the evidence that has been compiled and reviewed, may declare that a case exists for beatification, sometimes, but not always, a first step before canonization. In declaring a servant of God "blessed," the pope does not exercise infallibility but merely permits a local public cult to exist, whether at the level of a specific diocese, a nation, or a religious establishment. Canonization, on the other hand, is an expression of papal infallibility, and the universal church is required to believe that the servant of God "now reigns in eternal glory," and is thus "worthy of honor" by the universal church.

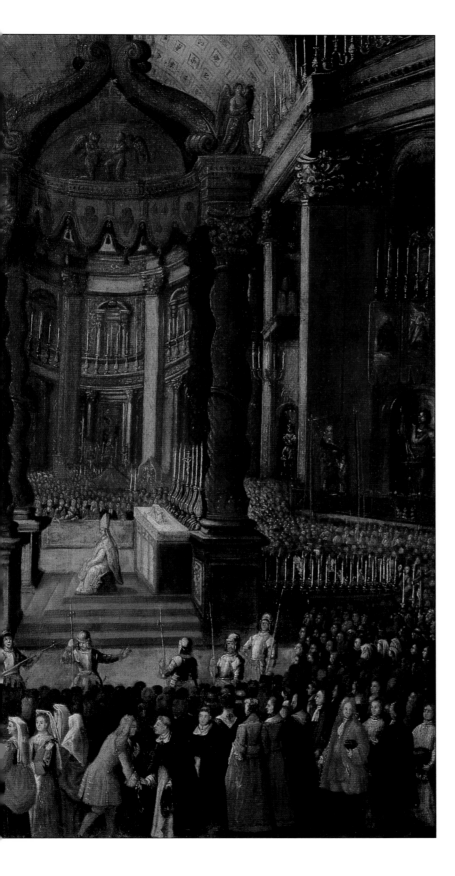

Many people believe that certain saints—the more "legendary," such as Christopher and George—were somehow "fired" by the Holy See in 1969. What happened is that those considered to be most historically questionable were given less prominence in the church calendars, but their sainthood—determined by the faithful—remains intact, as their cults do: witness the enduring popularity of Saint Christopher medals to protect travelers.

ABOVE: Less than a century after the event, Giotto's fresco in the Church of San Francesco in Assisi memorialized the Church's formal recognition of Francis's sainthood.

LEFT: This eighteenth-century painting documents Pope Innocent XIII presiding over a canonization in Saint Peter's Basilica.

THE HUMANITY OF SAINTS

Many of the saints in this collection are those with the most colorful legends, because these servants of God sparked the religious imaginations of countless people over hundreds of years, restoring the flame of faith, the beacon of hope, and the balm of charity in anguished hearts and doubting minds. These were people inspired by the love of God and their neighbors—the categories to which we have assigned them serve merely to highlight certain aspects of their service. To take only two examples, all the apostles, except John, to whom Christ entrusted Mary, are traditionally held to have been martyrs; Catherine of Siena, one of the Church's most celebrated mystics, was also intensely active in papal politics.

In his *Devil's Dictionary*, Ambrose Bierce gives us "*Saint, n.*, a sinner revised and edited." Saints were (and are) perfectly human. They were (and are) often boisterous, annoying, arrogant, impatient, intolerant, frightened, and rageful, as well as infinitely kind, open-hearted, good-humored, and compassionate. Sometimes slowly, sometimes suddenly, they surrendered their personalities to a greater love that turned human failings into human strengths: a passionate desire to serve, a fervent will to be a channel of the divine will. Their experience of heaven began here on earth—witnesses describe a radiance emanating from their faces, and joy is a recurrent theme in accounts of their lives, however beset they may have been by physical or spiritual torments.

Saints are venerated not because they are essentially different from us but because they are essentially the same—otherwise, we would turn from them in despair. Margaret beats the Devil, but then her curiosity drives her to chat with him. Christopher desires to do God's will, but he acknowledges his limitations; his confessor is wise enough to help Christopher find his humble place in the divine order.

The processes of canonization continue, tributes to transcendence. And all over the world, unknown saints are bridging the here and the hereafter, ushering in heaven on earth. Workaday angels and ordinary miracles are all around us, as long as we have the simplicity to see holiness in its countless daily manifestations of kindness, courage, generosity, integrity, and grace.

ABOVE: In the right-hand panel of a 1480 triptych by the Flemish painter Hans Memling, Barbara presents the tower in which she was imprisoned.

ABOVE: In the fifteenth-century Book of Hours, brave and good-humored Margaret—one of the most popular saints of the Middle Ages—defeats the Devil, here in dragon's guise.

CHAPTER ONE

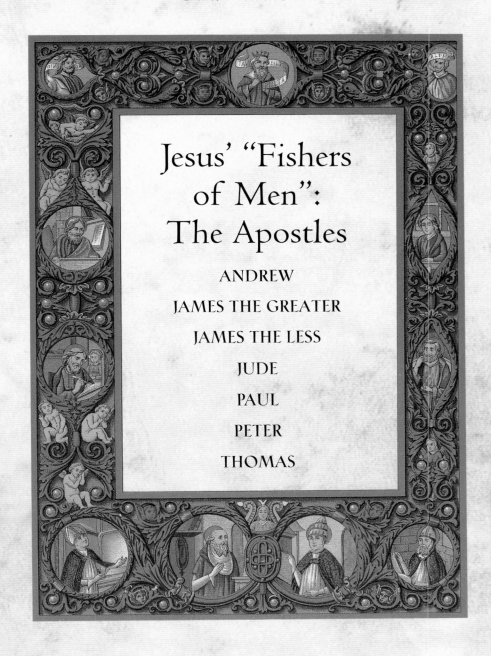

Jesus' "Fishers of Men": The Apostles

ANDREW

JAMES THE GREATER

JAMES THE LESS

JUDE

PAUL

PETER

THOMAS

THE APOSTLES WERE THE FIRST CHRISTIANS, THE FIRST TO RECOGNIZE JESUS' DIVINITY, AND THE FIRST TO CARRY JESUS' WORD TO THE WORLD AT LARGE. WHILE THERE WERE TWELVE APOSTLES IN ALL, WE HAVE SELECTED THESE SEVEN FOR THEIR INTRIGUING STORIES, WHICH REVEAL THEIR HUMANITY AS WELL AS THEIR SAINTLINESS.

ANDREW
NOVEMBER 30

Andrew, a fisherman on the Sea of Galilee, was the first to be called to leave all the trappings of his former life and go with Christ, heeding his call: "Follow me, I will make you fishers of men." For this reason, Andrew is always listed among the first four apostles, along with his brother Simon, later named Peter (page 26); James the Greater (page 22); and James' brother, John the Evangelist.

A number of tales are told of Andrew's ministry after the death of Christ, when the saint was already an old man. One such story illustrates that even saints make mistakes. Andrew learned that in the city of Nicaea seven devils were murdering folks at one of the city's gates. The apostle hurried to the place, and there commanded the demons to come out to him, which they did, in the form of dogs. He then ordered them to go away, and they did this, too. All those present converted to Christianity.

Andrew continued on his way and, arriving at the gates of another town, saw a funeral procession taking a young man to be buried. When the apostle asked how the young man had died, one of the mourners replied that seven dogs had killed him during the night. Andrew burst into tears when he realized that he had caused the young man's death, then asked the boy's father what he would give Andrew in return for his son's life. "I have nothing dearer than he," was the answer, "so I will give

him to thee." Through Andrew's intercession, the young man was restored to life and followed the apostle.

The last years of Andrew's ministry were in Achaea, in Greece, in the north of the Peloponnese. Around the year 60,

PAGES 18 AND 19: Perugino's Renaissance fresco The Giving of the Keys to Saint Peter, *of 1481-82, decorates the Vatican's Sistine Chapel.*

ABOVE: In this sixth-century mosaic from the Church of Sant'Apollinare Nuovo in Ravenna, Italy, Christ calls his first disciples, two humble fishermen, Andrew and his brother Simon (later called Peter).

Andrew was called to Patras, Greece, to defend his beliefs before Aegeus, the Roman proconsul of that province. Andrew reasoned with the proconsul in an attempt to convert him, but Aegeus only grew wrathful. However, his wife, Maximilla, accepted Christ and was baptized by the apostle, who persuaded her to adopt a life of chastity. Enraged by this, Aegeus ordered Andrew crucified, specifying that his hands and feet should be tied, not nailed, to the cross, in order to prolong his agony.

Andrew hung on the cross for two days, preaching the word of God and converting many. Moved by the patient suffering of the faithful old man, the people, even the unbelievers, began to demand that Aegeus bring Andrew down from the cross. Fearful of the angry crowd, Aegeus ordered that he be brought down, but Andrew prophesied that he would not come down alive. The apostle prayed fervently for release from the "heavy burden" of his body, the crowd saw him surrounded by a brilliant cloud of light, and when the cloud dissipated Andrew's soul went to God. Maximilla took his body away, prepared it for burial, and saw him interred. On his way home, Aegeus was attacked by a demon and died in the street.

According to one tradition, Andrew's relics were taken to the city of Saint Andrews in Scotland in the fourth century, and for this reason he is the patron saint of Scotland.

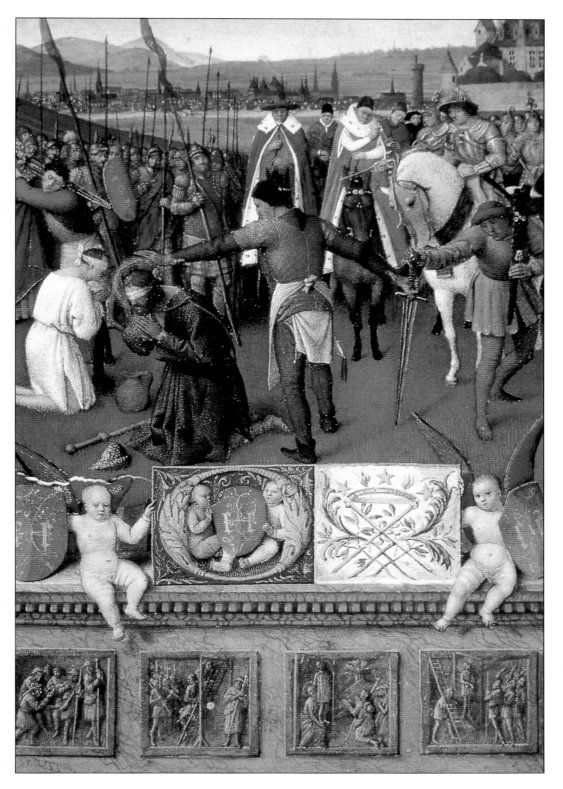

This jewel-like miniature from Jean Fouquet's 1455 Book of Hours for Étienne Chevalier shows the beheading of James the Greater, whose shrine at Compostela, Spain, still attracts pilgrims today.

JAMES THE GREATER
JULY 25

James and his brother John the Evangelist, sons of Zebedee, were both fishermen in what is now Israel and were among the first whom Jesus called to become "fishers of men." Jesus also selected the brothers, along with Peter, to be present at the Transfiguration, and so these three were preeminent among the apostles. James, known for the power—and loudness—of his preaching, was the first of the apostles to be martyred. (Jesus nicknamed the hot-tempered brothers "sons of thunder.")

Perhaps because Jesus had chosen him as a witness to a great mystery, James was associated in popular legend with magic. He was said to have gone to Spain to preach, but with little result; when he returned to Judea, the story goes, the Pharisees consulted a magician, Hermogenes, in order to publicly discredit James, and through him the doctrine of Christ. However, James argued so well against the magician's minion, Philetus, and performed so many miracles that Philetus not only accepted Christ but returned to his master and attempted to convert him as well. There ensued a battle of miracles and magic between James and Hermogenes, with the luckless Philetus as pawn. In the end, Hermogenes, too, was converted, and he brought his books of magic to James to be burned. But the apostle, concerned that the smoke from the unholy works might harm someone, commanded Hermogenes to throw them into the sea, which he did.

James was condemned to death by the provincial governor, Herod Agrippa I. The saint was beheaded in Jerusalem in 44, along with all the soldiers who formed his escort—who were converted by James en route to the place of execution. According to tradition, James' disciples took his body onto a boat with no rudder and set out to sea. They landed in Spain, and after many wonders and conversions, the saint's body was laid to rest at the famous shrine named for him, Santiago (Spanish for "Saint James")

de Compostela. Many miracles have been attributed to the saint's tomb. One man was so addicted to a sin that his bishop was in doubt about whether to absolve him; he sent the sinner to Compostela, telling him to write his sin on a piece of paper and place the paper on the saint's tomb. The man did so, praying passionately that his sin be forgiven, and in the morning he found that his prayers had been answered, and the paper was blank.

JAMES THE LESS
MAY 3

James the Less is so called to distinguish him from James the Greater, son of Zebedee, who was the elder of the two. James the Less, son of Alphaeus, is sometimes identified as "brother of the Lord" or, according to divergent traditions, as the stepbrother or cousin of Jesus. Jude was the brother of James the Less.

It is said that James the Less was so holy "from the very womb of his mother, that he never drank wine nor strong drink, nor ate meat" and was far from vain about his person. During the Crucifixion, James swore to eat nothing until Jesus rose from the

James the Less, a saint sometimes associated with sobriety, is shown in this Book of Hours of around 1435, above a drinking scene.

dead; shortly after the Resurrection, Jesus called for bread and gave it to James himself. James is also held to have been the first to say Mass in Jerusalem, by consensus of the disciples.

He was known as "the Just," and such was his reputation for sanctity that the Jews of Jerusalem, alarmed at the conversions all about them, went to James and demanded that he speak from atop the temple to the crowds gathering for Passover in the year 62. Such was the good opinion that the multitudes had of the bishop that it was believed that his word would surely bring the new converts back to Judaism. (It is unclear why the Jews went to a Christian known for his sanctity to bring converts back to Judaism. Perhaps they did not know of his faith but only of his goodness.)

James agreed, but once at the pinnacle of the temple, he professed his creed, to the joy of the Christians. The Scribes and Pharisees

Jude, a simple peasant, is shown holding a flail for threshing grain, in a sixteenth-century Book of Hours made by Simon Bening for the powerful German nobleman Albert of Brandenburg.

were so incensed that they climbed to the top of the temple and threw James to the ground, where he was stoned to death. The horrified crowd sought the murderers, but they had fled. In recognition of his holiness, James the Just was buried close to the temple where he had found martyrdom.

JUDE
OCTOBER 28

Also known as Thaddaeus, the apostle Jude, or Judas—"not Iscariot," as the Gospel says—is usually identified as a brother of his fellow apostle James the Less and sometimes of another apostle, Simon, as well. The Western tradition has it that Jude, celebrated by *The Golden Legend* for his "greatness of heart," was martyred in Persia together with Simon, and so the two are commemorated on the same day.

After the Ascension, the apostles set out on their missions. Thomas directed Jude to go to the court of Abgar, king of Edessa, a powerful city of Asia Minor (today southern Turkey), to fulfill a promise made in a letter from Christ to the king to heal him and instruct him. When Jude arrived at the king's court, Abgar recognized him as Christ's emissary by the divine radiance shining from the apostle's face. The illness that Abgar had beseeched Christ to cure was leprosy: Jude took Christ's letter and rubbed the king's face with it, whereupon Abgar was made whole. From Edessa, Jude traveled southeast into Mesopotamia (in modern-day Iraq), then north to Pontus, on the Black Sea, preaching and converting many. Simon, meanwhile, was in Egypt. The two are said to have reunited in Persia, making their way together to Babylonia, by the Persian Gulf.

In Babylonia, a certain military captain, preparing for war, learned that he was getting no answer from his gods about the expedition because of the presence of the apostles. He arranged a contest between the apostles and powerful magicians. Jude and Simon, filled with the truth of Christ, defeated the pagan mages but refused to allow them to be put to death, and at this everyone was filled with wonder at their virtue. In later contests, the apostles turned flesh-eating serpents back against the mages, but again saved their adversaries from death. They tamed two savage tigresses and performed other miracles of mercy in the name of Christ. They stayed fifteen months in that province, converting tens of thousands, including kings and princes.

The thwarted mages, filled with rage and spite, traveled to a neighboring city where pagan practices still ruled. There, the mages stirred up the priests and the people against the apostles. When Jude and Simon arrived, they were arrested and taken to the temple, where their very presence caused the demons to cry aloud in pain and fear from the mouths of the idols in which they dwelled. An angel appeared, giving the apostles a choice between the death of their oppressors or martydom; the two holy men chose to witness for their faith, so that souls might be saved.

Jude and Simon ordered the demons to come out and destroy the idols; this they did, and the furious priests descended upon the saints and killed them, but the king of the city removed their bodies to his city and built a great church in their honor. Like Rita of Cascia, Jude is a patron saint of desperate cases.

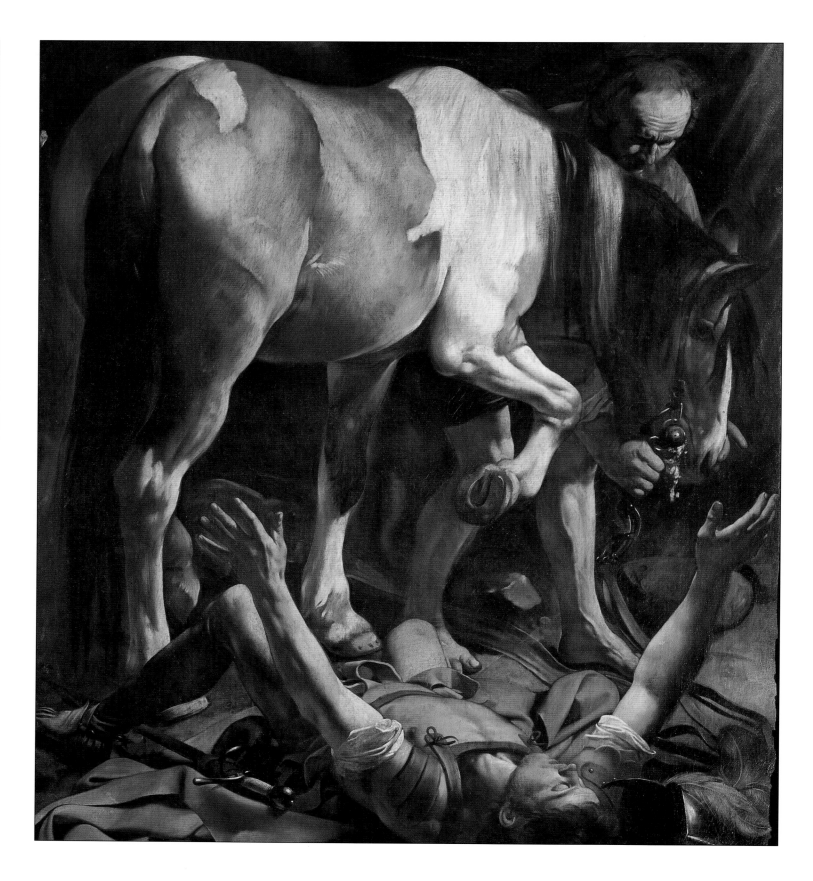

PAUL

JUNE 29, WITH PETER

Paul, one of the most energetic of the apostles, was born with the name Saul to a Jewish family of the bustling Cilician capital Tarsus, in what is today southern Turkey but was then one of the crossroads of the Roman Empire. Through his father, Saul enjoyed Roman citizenship and was raised as a Pharisee, receiving a thorough religious education in Jerusalem from the renowned Rabbi Gamaliel.

Saul was a tentmaker by trade, but his vocation was to root out Christians and deliver them to prison and death. He was on his way to Damascus for this purpose when he was blinded by a vision in which Jesus reprimanded him for persecuting the Christians and then told him that he, Saul, would spread the Christian faith among the Gentiles.

Saul took the name Paul, either from the Latin word for "small"—Paul described himself as "the least among the apostles"—or from the name of a Roman proconsul whom he converted. He traveled throughout the eastern Mediterranean and into Macedonia and Greece. As zealously as he had previously persecuted the followers of Jesus, so did he later establish Christian communities wherever he went, writing them the passionate, exhortatory letters that are so vivid a voice in the New Testament. Finally, he returned to Jerusalem, where he was arrested by the Roman governor for causing civil unrest.

Paul requested that he be tried at the emperor's court as a Roman citizen; in Rome, he was under house arrest for two years. The emperor in those days was Nero, and there are many tales of Paul and Peter defeating the imperial magician and converting many of the emperor's courtiers. Tradition also holds that Peter and Paul were martyred on the same day, but Paul may have been released, making several voyages, including one to Ephesus and perhaps one to Spain, before being arrested once more in Rome. Nero ordered that Paul, as a Roman citizen, be beheaded (which he was in the year 67) for the treasonable act of worshiping a greater king: the Christian God. Paul and Peter share a feast day, and the two—the ardent, intellectual Paul, and the hot-tempered, great-hearted Peter—are often depicted together.

OPPOSITE: The raw light and dark of Caravaggio's dramatic naturalism evoke the physical shock of Paul's spiritual awakening in this painting from the turn of the seventeenth century.

RIGHT: In a fresco of 1425-28 by Filippino Lippi, Paul exhorts his imprisoned fellow apostle Peter.

PETER

JUNE 29, WITH PAUL

Peter, whose original name was Simon, or Simeon, was, like his brother Andrew, a fisherman in Capernaum on the shores of the Sea of Galilee when he joined his brother at Jesus' behest to be among the "fishers of men." Jesus named Simon *Kephas*, the Aramaic word for "rock," saying, "Thou are *Kephas*, and upon this rock I will build my church." The Greek word for "rock" being *petros*, the first of Christ's apostles was thenceforth called, in the Greek-language Gospels, Simon Peter, or Peter.

Peter is one of the most vividly human of the saints—warm, spontaneous, and wholehearted. He was fearful, as when he thrice denied Jesus, but also deeply faithful and courageous, as when he voluntarily returned to Rome and certain martyrdom when he might have escaped. His wife, too, was martyred, and Peter's legend relates that as she was being led away, "he called her by name, and joyfully exclaimed: 'Dear wife, remember the Lord!'" In art as on their feast day, Peter is often paired with the educated, articulate, and equally passionate Paul.

Peter was the first of the apostles to be given the power of "binding and loosing," that is, of saying who would be saved and who would be damned. For this reason, Peter is typically shown with the keys of Heaven and is known popularly as the Heavenly Gatekeeper. The gift of spiritual healing may explain the tradition that Peter's very shadow could restore health.

Peter was also one of the apostles to whom it was vouchsafed to witness the mystery of the Transfiguration, and this may explain the overtones of sorcery in his legend, like those in the legend of James the Greater. Peter is supposed to have taken on Simon Magus, who sought to be worshiped as the Son of God. Simon was revered by the Roman people and was a favorite of the emperor Nero, but Peter countered his magical tricks and apparitions with reason and common sense.

One day, Simon Magus challenged Peter over the body of a dead youth: whichever of the two of them failed to bring the boy back to life would be executed. With his spells, Simon caused the dead boy's head to twitch, but Peter told the magician

Another fresco by Filippino Lippi shows Peter's crucifixion: the figure on the right seems to ask us what we would have done had we been present.

ABOVE: Filippino Lippi made himself a bystander (far right) at the contest between the apostles Peter and Paul and the emperor Nero's favorite sorcerer, Simon.

OPPOSITE: The scroll that Thomas holds in this fifteenth-century icon, from the Macedonian town of Ohrid, may refer to his famed stubborn rationality.

At the urging of the Christians of Rome, Peter made haste to quit the city, but at one of the gates the apostle saw Christ himself. Stunned, Peter asked him, *"Quo vadis Domine?"* (Lord, whither goest thou?) Jesus replied that he was going into the city to be crucified again. At that, Peter, weeping, declared that he would return, too, to be crucified with his Master. The vision of Christ vanished, and the apostle, knowing that his martyrdom was nigh, returned to the city. There, because he was not a Roman citizen, the Galilean fisher of men was condemned to be crucified, not beheaded as Paul was. Feeling unworthy of dying in the same position as Christ, Peter asked to be crucified head down; his request was granted, and he died in the year 64. According to tradition, he and Paul died on the same day, though in different places.

THOMAS
JULY 3

During Christ's lifetime, Thomas was one of the most unquestioning of the disciples, ready, even eager, to follow him to the death. Yet this apostle is known as Doubting Thomas because of his skepticism upon hearing of the resurrection. He is believed to have said, "Except I shall see in His hands the print of the nails, and put my finger in the place of the nails, and put my hand into His side, I will not believe."

After Christ invited his very human apostle to the proofs he had required, Thomas, falling to his master's feet, exclaimed, "My Lord and my God"—making Thomas the first to speak the divinity of Christ. Jesus did not rebuke his doubting follower but only remarked, "Because thou hast seen me, Thomas, thou hast believed. Blessed are they that have not seen, and have believed."

This may explain the tradition that Thomas went as a missionary to India, where he is said to be buried, and there relied on logical argument, rather than miracles, to persuade his doubtful hearers—those who had not seen—to believe.

to move away from the body, and immediately it was still. When Peter prayed in the name of the crucified Christ, the young man stood up and walked. The crowd gathered to stone the magician to death, according to his own terms for the wager, but Peter stopped them, saying, "Our Master teaches us to return good for evil."

One day, Simon Magus declared that Peter and Paul had insulted him, and that he would rise to heaven, having transcended the earthly realm. He indeed arose and flew about, and Nero, impressed, turned to Peter and Paul and accused them of being impostors. Whereupon Peter, in the name of Christ, commanded the angels of the Devil who were holding up Simon Magus to let go of him. Simon fell to the ground, broke his head open, and died. Nero, saddened by his loss, ordered that Peter and Paul be imprisoned; there the apostles converted the guards, who released them.

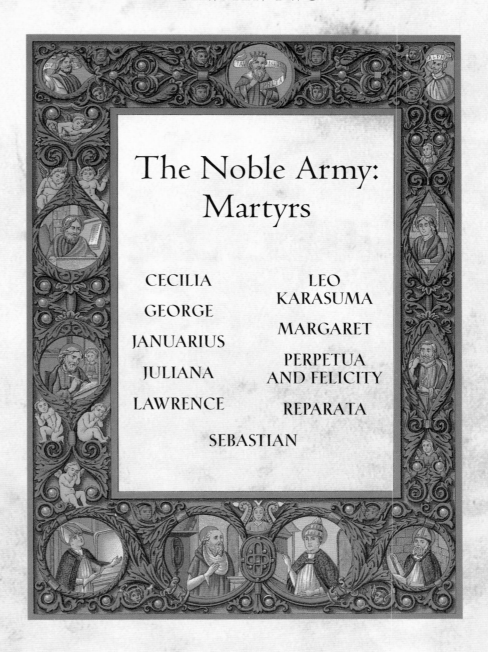

CHAPTER TWO

The Noble Army: Martyrs

CECILIA

GEORGE

JANUARIUS

JULIANA

LAWRENCE

LEO KARASUMA

MARGARET

PERPETUA AND FELICITY

REPARATA

SEBASTIAN

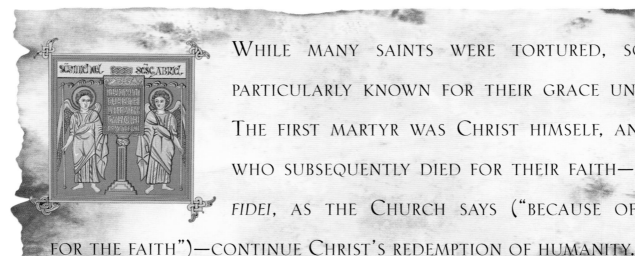

WHILE MANY SAINTS WERE TORTURED, SOME ARE PARTICULARLY KNOWN FOR THEIR GRACE UNDER FIRE. THE FIRST MARTYR WAS CHRIST HIMSELF, AND THOSE WHO SUBSEQUENTLY DIED FOR THEIR FAITH—*IN ODIUM FIDEI*, AS THE CHURCH SAYS ("BECAUSE OF HATRED FOR THE FAITH")—CONTINUE CHRIST'S REDEMPTION OF HUMANITY.

CECILIA
NOVEMBER 22

During the reign of the Roman emperor Marcus Aurelius, or perhaps Severus Alexander, there was a young Roman woman of noble birth, Cecilia, who was raised as a Christian and went about her daily affairs in constant communion with God, praying especially to remain a virgin. Despite this, her parents arranged for her to marry a young man, Valerian. When the wedding day came, Cecilia wore a hair shirt beneath a gown of gold cloth, and as the nuptial organs played, "she sang in her heart to God alone"—perhaps the reason why Cecilia is the patron saint of musicians.

When at last their friends and relations had left the young couple to themselves, Cecilia described a jealous, angelic lover, solemnly telling Valerian that he could see his rival only if he were baptized. For love of his bride, Valerian set off to find the hermit

PAGES 30 AND 31: This illustration from a French edition of The Golden Legend *shows angels bringing pestilence to an Italian town. The plague ceased when an altar to Saint Sebastian was built in Pavia.*

RIGHT: Lavinia Fontana, a fashionable portraitist in late sixteenth- and early seventeenth-century Rome, also created works for Pope Gregory XIII, such as this painting of Cecilia, who is identifiable by the organ in the background.

Urban, bishop of the Christian community, who was living in hiding in a cemetery outside the city. There, Valerian received a vision that convinced him to embrace Christianity. He returned home to Cecilia, and they were bound in a joyful spiritual union. Valerian's brother, Tiburtius, proved more obdurate, but Cecilia, reasoning with him, led him to see the light.

Valerian and Tiburtius served God in corporal works of mercy, especially in burying the saints martyred by the prefect Almachius. Upon discovering their works, the prefect commanded the brothers to answer for themselves; when they refused to acknowledge Jupiter as god, Almachius sent them into the custody of one Maximus, whom Valerian and Tibertius baptized, along with his entire household.

The following morning, heartened by Cecilia's fervent exhortations, they were all put to death; then Almachius, greedy for the brothers' estate, sent for Cecilia—who converted the soldiers he sent. The maiden held firm before the angry prefect, who ordered that she be boiled in a cauldron, wherein Cecilia remained miraculously cool. Almachius ordered that she be beheaded. The executioner delivered three strokes, which Cecilia survived, but by law he could not deliver a fourth. Cecilia lived three days more, during which time she gave away everything she owned to the poor, and asked Urban to consecrate her home as a church. This the bishop did, and he saw to it that the faithful Cecilia was buried in a place of honor.

GEORGE
APRIL 23

George, born in the third quarter of the third century to a noble family in Cappadocia, in what is today Turkey, was a handsome, high-ranking soldier of the Roman army. One day he found himself in Libya, at Silene, a town by a "deep lake as large as an ocean." In that lake there lived a hideous dragon, whose breath was deadly poison to anyone who came near, and the dragon coiled around the walls of the city.

For a time, the people of the city had placated the dragon with two sheep a day, but they had few sheep remaining and so had lately, in their desperation, fed it one sheep and a young person chosen by lottery. That day, the lot had fallen to the king's own daughter. His grief was great, and in vain he offered the people of the city riches in exchange for sparing his daughter, but they threatened to set fire to him, his house, and all he had if he did not abide by the law he himself had decreed.

George went to accompany the brave maiden, who bid him leave her, lest he share her fate, but George made the sign of the cross then charged the dragon, knocking it down. The maiden led the dragon to the city with her belt around its neck, "like a little dog on a leash." There, the knight made a bargain with the townspeople: he would kill the dragon if they would convert. This they did; George killed the dragon, and the king built a church that housed a spring "whose waters cured all languors."

In the meantime, the Roman emperors Diocletian and Maximian were executing many thousands of Christians, while many others, in terror, were renouncing Christ and sacrificing to the gods. George, his heart sore at this, resigned from the Roman army and confessed his faith publicly. The prefect, Dacian, commanded that George be seized and tortured, but at night God tenderly healed his wounds and lacerations "with His presence and His words."

The frustrated Dacian consulted a magician in an attempt to counteract what the prefect believed to be the spells of the Christians. Twice, the magician offered George a goblet of poisoned wine, and twice George made the sign of the cross before the goblet, drank the wine, and remained unharmed. The magician fell to his knees, pleaded for the saint's forgiveness, converted to Christianity, and was himself beheaded by Dacian's executioners.

Against a background of peace and civilization, this grotesque dragon, a nightmarish cave creature, is defeated by a knight in shining armor—George—in Paolo Uccello's mid-fifteenth-century painting.

Dacian attempted another tack entirely, offering George rich rewards if he would honor the pagan gods in their temple. George smilingly agreed, and the city was adorned in celebration, as crowds gathered by the place of worship. The saint entered, knelt, and prayed to God. Flames rained down from the skies, destroying temple, statues, and priests; the yawning ground engulfed all the rest, leaving George unscathed.

When Dacian's own wife became a Christian, he had her beaten, but her only fear was that she would die unbaptized. George reassured her that "the outpouring of thy blood will be thy Baptism." The following day, Dacian ordered that George be hauled through the city streets and then beheaded. George prayed that all those who invoked his name should be helped, and this was granted.

George was the Crusaders' patron saint, appearing several times in visions leading heavenly hosts.

JANUARIUS
SEPTEMBER 19

Januarius was born in Naples or nearby Benevento, Italy; he was almost certainly bishop of Benevento. During the persecutions of the Roman emperor Diocletian in the third century, two deacons, Sossus and Proculus, and two laypersons, Euticius and Acutius, were arrested and imprisoned. Januarius very much admired Sossus, and so, despite the danger of doing so, he went to visit him in prison. Januarius was eventually arrested, along with Festus, his deacon, and Desiderius, a lector; they were all tortured and then imprisoned along with their four fellow martyrs.

They were sentenced to be thrown to wild animals in the local amphitheater, but when the time came the starving beasts would not touch them but were as docile as pets. The saints were accused of being magicians, but they responded with continued confessions of their Christian faith. Finally, they were beheaded in Pozzuoli, Italy, in 305.

OPPOSITE: Wearing his bishop's miter and accompanied by his bishop's crozier, Januarius is represented in glory, among the communion of saints, in the presence of God. The cherub in the lower right carries a reliquary containing the celebrated vial said to hold the saint's blood.

Januarius—or, more familiarly, Gennaro—is the patron saint of Naples, where his relics have rested for some centuries now. Among these relics is a head alleged to be that of the saint, and, most famously, a vial said to contain a small quantity of the saint's blood. For five hundred years, a phenomenon known as liquefaction has taken place: the dark and solid substance in the vial becomes red and liquid. Other similar manifestations, relative to other saints' relics, have been explained, but this one has not.

The Church is reluctant to confirm this as a miracle—the phenomenon takes place erratically, under different circumstances, and in different degrees—but perhaps the very limitations of human explanation themselves serve as a powerful invitation to humility before the mysteries that exist between heaven and earth.

JULIANA
FEBRUARY 16

Juliana was a Christian, the daughter of a highly placed pagan family of Nicomedia, today Izmit, near Istanbul. She was betrothed to Eulogius, the prefect of the city, but refused to consummate the nuptials unless he became a Christian, too. This he would not do. Juliana's father, incensed at his daughter's willfulness, had her stripped and beaten, then gave her to her intended. Eulogius, however, spoke to her cajolingly, calling her "sweet Juliana," and asking her why she had turned cold. Juliana repeated her demand, at which Eulogius admitted he feared for his life should he profess Christianity. Juliana exclaimed, "If thou art in such fear of a mortal emperor, how much greater must be my fear of my Emperor, who is eternal!"

At that, Eulogius ordered his men to beat and torture Juliana, but she remained unhurt, so he had her bound in chains and imprisoned. In prison, Juliana was visited by a demon disguised as an angel, who, in soft tones, counseled Juliana to adore the pagan gods because "the Lord has taken pity upon thee, and is disposed to spare thee a cruel agony and a frightful death." In anguished confusion, Juliana prayed to know God's true will; she was told to shake the truth out of her visitor. Juliana grabbed the angel, who confessed that he was a demon, sent by his father to tempt Juliana. When the girl asked the name of the demon's father, he answered, "He is Beelzebub, who compels us

to evil, and beats us cruelly whenever the Christians have the best of us. So I shall pay dearly for this day, since I have failed to conquer thee!" Juliana tied the demon's hands, hurled him down, then struck him with her chains, ignoring the demon's pleas for mercy.

When Eulogius had Juliana brought out of prison, he was amazed at the sight of her dragging the demon behind her. In vain, the cursed creature cried, "Lady Juliana, do not any longer make a laughingstock of me, or never again shall I be able to have power over a Christian! Christians are said to be merciful, and yet thou hast not the least pity for me!" But Juliana hauled the demon around the public square, then finally tossed him into a public toilet.

Juliana's erstwhile fiancé had her stretched on a wheel until her very bones broke, but a holy angel shattered the wheel and healed her. At this, all the onlookers were converted—and immediately beheaded. After further tortures that left the saint unharmed, Eulogius commanded that Juliana, too, be beheaded. As she was led to the scaffold, the demon appeared, taunting her and urging on the executioners, but at a glance from Juliana he fled in terror.

After Juliana's death, a noble lady took her body back to Italy and had it buried in Naples.

OPPOSITE: Looking both contemplative and stern enough to shake the truth out of a hundred demons, Juliana stands by the Virgin and Child in Andrea Mantegna's late-fifteenth-century painting.

ABOVE: In his 1636 painting of Lawrence, the Spanish painter Francisco de Zurbarán emphasized the saint's earthy, physical nature.

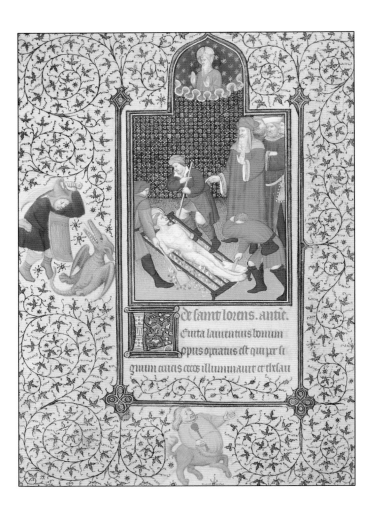

The thirteenth-century Book of Hours of François, duc de Guise, portrays the jocular Lawrence on the grill that was the instrument of his torture.

LAWRENCE

AUGUST 10

Lawrence was a deacon of Rome, charged with authority over one of seven ecclesiastical sections. He was devoted to Pope Saint Sixtus II, who, in the year 258, upon becoming aware that he was about to be imprisoned by the emperor Valerian, called Lawrence and told him to distribute the Church's treasures to the poor before the riches could be confiscated by the emperor. Lawrence did so and, in the course of his almsgiving, is said to have healed a number of people, and especially to have restored sight to the blind.

As the Holy Father had predicted, the imperial troops came to Lawrence, demanding the riches of the Church. The deacon gathered around him the destitute and the helpless of the neighborhood, and said, "Behold, the treasure thou seekest is an everlasting one!"

Lawrence was subjected to grievous torments by Valerian's soldiers but, buoyed by thoughts of Heaven, smiled radiantly throughout, so that his captor accused him of using witchcraft not to feel the pain. Finally, his legend relates, the emperor ordered Lawrence grilled, but the deacon only continued to beam, even joking, "Turn me over, I'm done on this side!" With this, it is said that he gave his soul to God (though he more likely was beheaded).

In Italy, the night of Saint Lawrence is traditionally the night of shooting stars. Lawrence is the patron saint of archivists and comedians, among others.

LEO KARASUMA

FEBRUARY 6

(WITH THE MARTYRS OF JAPAN)

In the two years of his mission to Japan, from 1549 to 1551, Francis Xavier (p. 78) made many converts. Other Jesuits came in his wake, as did Franciscan missionaries, and so effective were these preachers that it is estimated that within fewer than forty years some two hundred thousand Japanese people were professed Christians.

In 1585, the emperor of Japan named Toyotomi Hideyoshi—a humble peasant's son who by his military genius and statesmanship had achieved the confidence of the emperor—*kampaku*, or chief minister. The emperor was essentially a figurehead; it was Hideyoshi who effectively ruled the nation, which in the next few years he unified and guided toward peace and prosperity. Nevertheless, in 1588, fearing the influence of the Jesuits, Franciscans, and native Christians, Hideyoshi gave the missionaries six months to leave the country. Although many obeyed, others stayed, and went into hiding, as, curiously, were their brethren half a world away in England at almost the same time.

In 1589, Karasuma, a Korean in Japan, was baptized Leo by Jesuits; prior to his conversion, he had been a pagan priest. He became a Franciscan tertiary, that is, a layman observing a part of the rule of the Friars Minor, and was the leader of the local converts, active in teaching.

In 1596, a Spanish ship's captain publicly boasted that the secret purpose of the Christian missionaries was to prepare the way for a Portuguese or Spanish conquest of Japan. Hideyoshi now began to aggressively persecute the Christians, beginning with a group of twenty-six that included Leo Karasuma. In 1597, most of them suffered mutilated ears; their faces bloody, they were taken to a place near Nagasaki and bound to crosses. At a signal, their executioners raised their spears and killed the martyrs, which included Leo's brother and his twelve-year-old nephew, an altar boy. The Christians around them gathered their clothing and their blood, to which miracles were attributed. These were the first martyrs of Japan. Two later groups subsequently were canonized.

MARGARET

JULY 20

Margaret, martyred during the reign of Diocletian, was one of the most popular saints of the Middle Ages—hers was one of the voices heard by Joan of Arc (p. 88). She was born in Antioch (whose ruins lie in modern-day Turkey), where her father, Theodosius, was a nobleman and high priest of a pagan cult. He came to hate his daughter when Margaret, after receiving the Christian faith through her nurse, was baptized upon reaching the age of reason.

One day when Margaret, now fifteen and exceedingly beautiful, was watching her father's sheep with some other maidens, a Roman prefect, Olybius, happened by. Smitten with the young girl's great loveliness, Olybius ordered his servants to abduct her, intending to marry her if she were free, or make her his concubine if she were a slave. At his home, he had Margaret brought to him for questioning; on learning that she was Christian, Olybius was shocked that "a damsel so fair and noble should have for god one that was crucified."

The fearless Margaret began to reason with the prefect, hoping to convert him, but to no avail. Enraged, Olybius ordered her imprisoned. The next morning, he pleaded with her, for her beauty's sake, to worship the pagan gods, but she refused. When he threatened her with torture and death, she, who had never known anything but the comforts of wealth and the love of her friends, replied joyfully that she wished nothing more than to die for Christ, who had died for her. Even as she suffered the agonies of the rack, she exulted in the salvation of her soul.

Once more in prison, Margaret prayed that her adversary be made visible. Instantly a dreadful dragon appeared and swallowed her whole. She made the sign of the cross, causing the apparition to burst, and escaped. Then the Devil appeared to her as a handsome young man who took her hand and pleaded, "Torment me no more!" But Margaret grabbed him by the head, knocked him down, and set her foot on him, declaring him defeated.

Her curiosity had always been lively, and she would not let the Devil go until he explained to her why he harassed the Christians so. First, explained Satan, he detested goodness, envying those who had the "blessedness which he himself had lost." And second, he said, Solomon had bottled up a number of demons in a vase; after he died, however, flames issuing from the vase caught the

attention of greedy men, who thought there might be something of value inside. Alas, when they smashed the vase, they gained nothing, and the demons were loosed upon the world. Margaret raised her foot and sent the Devil packing with an energetic kick in the rump.

The next morning, she again refused to sacrifice, and again she was tortured; this time she was set afire then plunged into a tub of water, which miraculously shattered. When Margaret stepped out unharmed, "five thousand persons were converted, and were beheaded for professing the name of Christ." But the furious and frustrated Olybius was not one of them, and in order to forestall more conversions, he commanded that the maiden be beheaded instantly. Margaret asked for and was granted time to say a prayer. She prayed for herself and her tormentors, and for those who would ask her help in the future—in particular, women in labor, whose patron saint she is.

PERPETUA AND FELICITY
MARCH 7

Perpetua and Felicity were two of six saints martyred together in Carthage, Africa, in the year 203, during the reign of the Roman emperor Septimius Severus. Vibia Perpetua was a wellborn young wife with a child she was still nursing; Felicity was a slave in the last stages of pregnancy. The two women, with the Romans Secundulus, Saturninus, and Revocatus, also a slave, were catechumens, that is, still receiving religious instruction; they were baptized when already under arrest, along with a certain Saturus, and Perpetua's little child was taken from her.

The six Christians were remanded to the city jail, where Perpetua had her first vision, or dream, of a narrow golden ladder, at the foot of which was coiled a terrifying dragon. Saturus, who had been baptized first, climbed up the ladder first, encouraging his sisters and brothers in Christ to follow. At that, Perpetua knew that they would all be martyred. When Perpetua's pagan father

Margaret, with other maidens, seems to be engaged in religious discussion with the Roman prefect, as her father's sheep peacefully graze.

visited her, his shame, rage, and bafflement grieved her, and the loss of her baby caused her great sorrow.

After the six were condemned to be given to wild beasts in the arena, Perpetua had more dreams, including one in which she bested Satan in physical combat. (In Saturus' vision in prison, Heaven was a place of lightness of heart.)

In jail, Felicity gave birth to a baby girl, who was adopted by a Christian family. So painful was the delivery that a guard tauntingly asked, how would Felicity manage in the arena, if she was already suffering so much?

The martyrs entered the arena "with gay and gallant looks," the elegant Perpetua arranging her hair as if for a social engagement. She and Felicity supported each other, as famished wild beasts attacked the friends in Christ. In the end, they exchanged the kiss of peace before the executioners stabbed them in the throat. Perpetua did not die at once, but in her agony, pointed the sword herself for the second, fatal thrust.

Perpetua wrote part of her group's story of martyrdom, while Saturus wrote a second part; the author of the rest remains unknown.

REPARATA
OCTOBER 8

Reparata is believed to have been martyred during the reign of the Roman emperor Decius in the third century. Her legend relates that she was a bright, vivacious girl of only twelve years of age, in Caesarea, the Roman capital of Palestine, in present-day Israel. She was betrayed for being a Christian to the prefect, who, moved by her youth and beauty, tried to save her from death by gently dissuading her from her faith. Reparata, however, was simple and strong in her belief and roundly disputed the prefect's arguments. The prefect, thwarted in his good intentions, sent the girl to be tortured, but she remained steadfastly cheerful and serenely certain of salvation.

Next, the prefect had her thrown into a furnace, where, untouched by the flames, she joyfully sang hymns to the glory of God. Once more, the prefect invited her to worship the pagan idols, and once more, from inside the furnace, the child refused. Exasperated, the prefect ordered that she be taken away and

beheaded. His order was carried out, but Reparata never ceased singing until her head was separated from her body.

The saint's cult continues to this day, perhaps because her spiritual nature so exemplified the childlike qualities Christ recommended to his disciples.

SEBASTIAN
JANUARY 20

Sebastian, it is said, was born in the city of Narbonne, in the south of France, and lived in Milan until, in the early fourth century, the pagan emperors Diocletian and Maximian appointed the handsome young soldier head of the First Cohort and took him into the imperial entourage.

After a period of religious tolerance, the emperors began a particularly vicious persecution of Christians in 303. Sebastian used his position in the army to hearten his co-religionists as they faced martyrdom. Tales tell of his converting many of those who witnessed his unshakable faith, including the prefect of Rome, whom he healed of a chronic illness, and the prefect's son and household.

Another prefect, however, denounced Sebastian as a Christian to Diocletian. The emperor, in a rage, accused his favorite of betraying him. Sebastian replied, "For thee and for the State of Rome I have always prayed to God Who is in Heaven!" But Diocletian ordered him tied to a stake in the Field of Mars, an area dedicated to the pagan god of war. There, the imperial archers shot Sebastian with arrows until the shafts were as thick, it is said, as spines upon a hedgehog; then they left him for dead.

Some days later, Sebastian, miraculously whole, appeared before the imperial palace to upbraid the emperors for their cruelty toward the Christians. This time, Diocletian and Maximian ordered Sebastian's fellow soldiers to beat him to death and commanded that his body be tossed into the *cloaca*, or sewer, so that no one might find it and honor it. But Sebastian came to Saint Lucina in a dream; he told her where to find his body and asked her to bury it "at the feet of the Apostles" on the Appian Way.

OPPOSITE: Sebastian can be recognized by the arrow he holds and by his great beauty, exquisitely represented by Raphael around 1503.

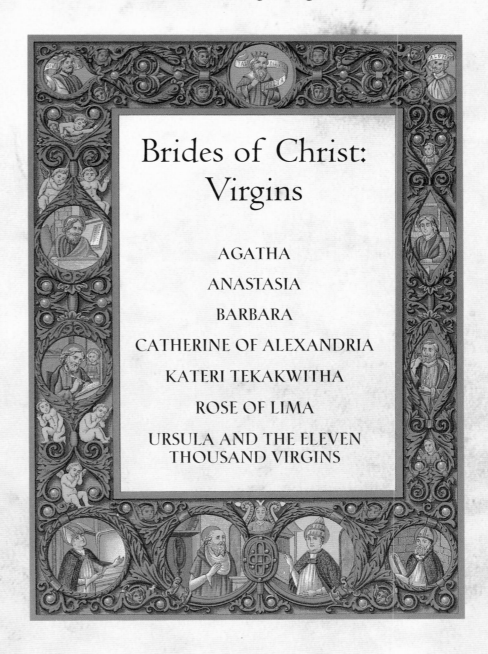

Chapter Three

Brides of Christ: Virgins

AGATHA

ANASTASIA

BARBARA

CATHERINE OF ALEXANDRIA

KATERI TEKAKWITHA

ROSE OF LIMA

URSULA AND THE ELEVEN
THOUSAND VIRGINS

CHRIST PRAISED THOSE WHO REMAINED CELIBATE BECAUSE THEY COULD MORE FULLY PURSUE THE SPIRITUAL LIFE. THIS WAS ESPECIALLY TRUE FOR WOMEN, WHOSE HOUSEHOLD RESPONSIBILITIES LEFT THEM LITTLE TIME FOR RELIGION. AS VIRGINS BECAME "BRIDES OF CHRIST," THEIR HONOR GREW. WHILE REMAINING CELIBATE IS FAR FROM THEIR ONLY QUALIFICATION FOR SAINTHOOD, IT ENABLED THESE SAINTS TO PURSUE HIGHER GLORY IN OTHER WAYS.

AGATHA

FEBRUARY 5

Agatha, a third-century native of Catania, in Sicily, was nobly born, wealthy, exceedingly beautiful, and devoted to Christ, having been consecrated to God from her earliest years. One Quintianus, consul of Sicily under the Roman emperor Decius, sought to marry her for reasons as corrupt as he was: prestige, riches, lust—and the desire to bring her down to the worship of idols.

Outspoken and immovable, Agatha refused, whereupon Quintianus sent her to a woman named Aphrodisia, a madam who lived steeped in transgression with her nine wicked daughters. Aphrodisia and her daughters harassed Agatha night and day, first menacing her, then attempting to seduce her into the innumerable byways of sin. Agatha, strong in her convictions, turned aside both flattery and threats, gently affirming her faith. Aphrodisia conceded defeat, reporting to Quintianus: "It were easier to soften stone, or to turn iron into lead, than to turn this girl's soul away from Christ!"

Quintianus summoned Agatha, but her answers to his interrogation only angered him and wounded his pride, so he ordered that she be imprisoned. The next day, he again ordered her to

PAGES 46 AND 47: As Catherine of Alexandria prays, the wheel intended for her martyrdom explodes, in this center panel of a triptych of 1506 by Lucas Cranach the Elder. The Saint Catherine's Wheel firework is named for the saint's symbol.

ABOVE: This miniature from a 1400 French edition of The Golden Legend *illustrates the martyrdom of Agatha. Female saints were—and are—often subjected to torments specific to their sex.*

renounce Christ, and again Agatha refused, her suffering face alight with joy. Quintianus commanded that Agatha be placed on the rack and her breasts tortured and finally torn off; that night, Peter (p. 26) appeared to Agatha in a vision and healed her after the torture. For this reason, Agatha is often shown holding a tray with breasts on it.

The next day, the consul ordered yet another torment, but an earthquake interrupted the proceedings. The frightened people began to murmur against Quintianus, saying that his injustice was endangering the city. Fearful, the consul imprisoned Agatha yet again. In her cell, with Heaven so near, she prayed one last time, crying out loudly to God to take her soul, whereupon the faithful maiden breathed her last.

ANASTASIA

DECEMBER 25

The persecutions initiated by the Roman emperors Diocletian and Maximian extended throughout the empire, including Maximian's home province of Pannonia, an area along the Danube in present-day Hungary and Serbia. In Sirmium (today Sremska Mitrovica, Serbia), one of the chief cities of that province, a Christian woman named Anastasia was martyred in 304. Today she is still commemorated in the Byzantine calendar, but there is no trace in the Roman Catholic roster of this saint, who was once popular in western Europe as well as in the East.

Traditionally, Anastasia is held to have been born to one of the wealthiest and highest-ranking families in Rome, the daughter of a pagan father, Praetaxatus, and a Christian mother, Faustina. Anastasia received her faith from her mother and from Saint Chrysogonus, who would prove a mainstay during her tribulations, beginning with a marriage imposed upon her by her father.

Anastasia had made a vow of chastity, and to keep it in the face of her corrupt pagan husband's importunities, she pretended

Anastasia—the figure on the left, in red—appears in the Byzantine calendar and in works of the Eastern Empire such as this fifteenth-century Russian icon. The youngest daughter of the last czar of Russia was undoubtedly named for this immensely popular saint.

to be sick. In secret, however, and disguised in shabby robes, she continued her practice of comforting jailed Christians. When Publius, her husband, found out that she was well, he imprisoned her and began to starve her to death slowly in order to gain her dowry, which he was already spending on shameful pastimes, as Anastasia wrote to Chrysogonus.

Instead, Publius died, whereupon the emperor gave Anastasia, a prize of breeding and wealth, to another prefect, on condition that the prefect force her to sacrifice to the gods. As Anastasia's second husband was about to have sex with her, he was struck blind; when he went to the temple to pray to the gods to restore his sight, his demon gods only jeered at him: "Because thou didst wish to ravish Anastasia, who is a saint, thou hast been delivered to us, to be tortured with us forever in Hell." And, indeed, the man died on his way home.

In the end, Anastasia was taken, imprisoned again, and once more left to starve, this time by imperial decree, but Saint Theodora sent her manna from Heaven for two months, after which, according to legend, the authorities took Anastasia, with

two hundred other virgins, to Palmaria, an island whose name recalls the palm of martyrdom that in art distinguishes those who have died for their faith. There, the local prefect ordered that Anastasia be tied to a stake and burned alive, and so she passed to her reward.

BARBARA

DECEMBER 4

Under the reign and persecutions of the Roman emperor Maximian, there lived a very wealthy pagan, Dioscorus, who had a daughter so beautiful that he shut her up in a very tall tower so that no potential suitor could see her. Nevertheless, Dioscorus was approached by so many princes asking for his daughter's hand that he finally went to her and asked what her will was in the matter.

Barbara, although she was still a catechumen being instructed in preparation for her baptism, was fervently dedicated to chastity. She angrily rejected even the idea of marriage, and Dioscorus went away on a long journey. One day, Barbara left her tower to oversee a bathhouse that her father was having built; finding that he had ordered only two windows to be made, she told the builders to add a third one in honor of the Holy Trinity. (For this reason, she is the patron saint of architects.) She moved into the bathhouse, was baptized there, and—emulating John the Baptist (p. 91) in the desert—lived for a time on "honeysuckle and locusts."

After a time, Barbara returned to her tower. Seeing the idols that her father worshiped, she was suddenly made full of the Holy Spirit "and became marvelously subtle and clear in the love of Jesus Christ, for she was environed with the grace of God Almighty, of sovereign glory and pure chastity."

Dioscorus returned. Discovering three windows in the bathhouse where he had ordered two, he summoned Barbara to answer for it. When she replied that the three windows stood for the Father, the Son, and the Holy Spirit, Dioscorus, enraged, drew his sword to kill his daughter, who was miraculously carried up to a mountaintop. Undeterred, her father dragged her down from the mountain by her hair, imprisoned her, and denounced her to the imperial authorities. When the judge offered her a choice between sacrificing to the gods and dying "by cruel torments," Barbara joyously affirmed her faith.

Like many northern painters, the Flemish master Robert Campin was fond of creating detailed interiors—particularly apt for Barbara, imprisoned in her tower. The bathhouse she redesigned is visible outside the window.

After she was tortured, Barbara was comforted by a holy vision; in the end, she was condemned to death. Dioscorus himself took Barbara to a mountaintop, where she prayed to God "that Thou wilt not remember their sins, for Thou knowest our fragility." A voice assured her that her prayers were heard, and so Barbara has remained the protector of all those who might die unshriven, that is, without the sacraments. Her own father beheaded her; when he came down from the mountain, he was destroyed by lightning, and this is why Barbara is also the patron saint of gunners and miners—two groups engaged in explosive occupations.

terrible engine of torture was devised, a huge series of armed wheels that would tear the young girl to pieces (this device gave its name to the firework called Saint Catherine's Wheel and is her symbol).

Catherine prayed and the wheel burst asunder, so powerful was her faith. The queen came forward and rebuked her husband, the emperor, who had his wife taken away, maimed, and killed. The next day, the emperor's captain and his soldiers confessed their faith, and they, too, were martyred. The emperor summoned Catherine one last time, accusing her of witchcraft and demanding

CATHERINE OF ALEXANDRIA

NOVEMBER 25

In the fourth century, the Roman emperor Maxentius, or perhaps Maximinus, called all the people to Alexandria (in present-day Egypt) to sacrifice to the gods. The Christians refused, and the emperor ordered that they be tortured. Catherine, who had remained at her wealthy Roman father's palace in the city, heard the awful sounds, and set out to learn the truth of the matter. She found some Christians suffering hideous punishments, while others, in terror of their fellows' pain, had submitted to the emperor and were worshiping the pagan idols.

Not fearlessly, but with great courage, Catherine courteously addressed the emperor in Latin, learnedly and at length, following which she reverted to "the common speech." The emperor was impressed despite himself with "the keenness of her mind and the beauty of her body," though she was "but a frail woman." Unable to defeat her arguments, he summoned the fifty wisest philosophers to Alexandria, but she defeated them, too.

The emperor sought to make her one of his wives, and when Catherine, pledged to Christ, refused, he had her thrown in prison to starve. There, Catherine converted the queen and the emperor's captain of the guard, and a white dove, recalling the emblem of the Holy Spirit, fed her. Upon her release, Catherine again refused the king, and a

Catherine's open book recalls her great learning, and wheels decorate her crown of martyrdom in this detail from the Dutch artist Gerard David's Virgin and Saints.

that she give up her religion or die. One last time, Catherine refused, as simple and steadfast in her faith as she was "admirable in her wisdom." As she went to her death, she prayed that those who commemorated her passion or invoked her name might find mercy. Her prayers were answered, and when she was beheaded, milk, not blood, flowed from her neck, and angels carried her twenty days' journey away, to Mount Sinai, where wonders took place at her tomb.

KATERI TEKAKWITHA

JULY 14

The Blessed Kateri Tekakwitha was the daughter of a Mohawk chief and an Algonquin Christian who had been captured by an Iroquois and given in marriage to him. The Mohawk village of Ossernenon (today Auriesville, New York), where Kateri Tekakwitha was born in 1656, had been the scene of the martyrdom of several French Jesuits and laymen some ten years earlier. During her childhood, an epidemic of smallpox damaged Kateri's eyesight and marred her face; worse still, her parents and a brother died in the onslaught, leaving the girl virtually alone. In 1676, instructed by Father Jacques de Lamberville, another Jesuit missionary, Kateri became a Catholic, incurring the enmity of her remaining family and of others in the village.

Aware of the martyrdom suffered by missionaries in that very village, Kateri knew that she was in danger, and her soul craved the spiritual nurturing she could only find among others of her new faith. The year after her baptism, Kateri made her way north, walking some two hundred miles to Caughnawaga, Canada, one of the recent Christian Indian settlements near Montreal, where she made her first communion that Christmas.

In 1679, Kateri, who would come to be known as the Lily of the Mohawk, took a vow of chastity; she already enjoyed a reputation for holiness and selflessness as well as for a number of miracles occurring through her intercession. She died the following year, on April 17. Three hundred years later, Pope John Paul II beatified her; she is the first Native North American to be put forward for canonization.

ROSE OF LIMA

AUGUST 23

Isabel de Flores y del Oliva, born in 1586 and known and confirmed as Rose—by Saint Toribio, archbishop of Lima— was the daughter of Spaniards in Lima, Peru. The beautiful Rose was so fearful, not only of sin but of being the occasion of sin, that she nearly disfigured herself in order to diminish her attractiveness. In time, she grew to understand that it was her attitudes that required discipline as much as or even more than her outward appearance, and so she labored spiritually to attain humility.

When Rose's parents lost almost everything they had in a failed investment, the hardworking young woman gardened by day, raising flowers to sell, then embroidered and did other needlework at night. She was content in her work and in her obedience, though she did not shrink from speaking her mind when she was moved to do so. For ten years, she refused to marry, finally taking a vow of chastity. She became a Dominican tertiary and a recluse, secluding herself in a small outbuilding in her family's garden.

Inspired by a desire to emulate the sufferings of Christ, Rose imposed physical penances upon herself; at times these were extreme enough to warrant the attention not only of relatives and neighbors but of the ecclesiastical authorities as well. At the same time, following the injunction of Christ, she performed corporal works of mercy, caring for the sick of the despised lower classes. Throughout her short life, which ended in 1617, she glowed with a radiant manifestation of her love for God, which was most visible when she received Holy Communion.

Rose was the first person born in the Americas to be canonized, and she is one of the patron saints of South America.

OPPOSITE: Giovanni Battista Tiepolo, one of the great Venetian painters, produced an imposing architectural fresco of the Virgin and Child with three Dominican saints: Rose of Lima, Catharine of Siena, and Agnes of Montepulciano. Rose and Agnes were both canonized in Tiepolo's lifetime.

URSULA AND THE ELEVEN THOUSAND VIRGINS

OCTOBER 21

Ursula, the Christian daughter of a lesser Christian king in Britain, "shone with such wisdom, such beauty, and such holiness of life, that her fame took wing, and became known everywhere." The great king himself proposed a marriage between Ursula and his son, forwarding his purpose with both blandishments and threats. Ursula, pledged to God, devised a ruse to delay the marriage and bring numerous souls to Christ: she asked that Ethereus, her betrothed, receive instruction in the Christian faith and be baptized. In the meantime, he was to provide Ursula with ten virgin companions; each of the eleven virgins would be assigned one thousand maidens.

Ethereus converted wholeheartedly and ordered that all of Ursula's conditions be met. The princess and her eleven thousand attendants made their way to Cologne, where an angel foretold that Ursula would return to that city and be martyred there. As Ursula and her retinue traveled to Rome, she gradually converted her maidens; once in Rome, other holy men and women, including Pope Cyriacus himself, joined their journey to martyrdom.

They made their way back to Cologne, where Julian, the wicked prince of the Huns, awaited, forewarned by captains of the Roman guard. Ethereus received an angelic command telling him to fly to Cologne to share his beloved's fate. The throng of Christians arrived, and "when the barbarians saw them, they fell upon them with a tremendous shout, and, like wolves raging among the sheep, put the whole multitude to death." Only Urusula was spared; the prince, "dumfounded at her wondrous beauty," sought to make her his wife, but Ursula refused. In a fury of frustrated pride, the prince himself shot her with an arrow, and so she passed to her reward.

Artist Hans Memling placed an elegant dog at Ursula's feet to symbolize her steadfast faith in the face of imminent death at the hands of a Hun prince, identified by the tents of his nomadic people behind him.

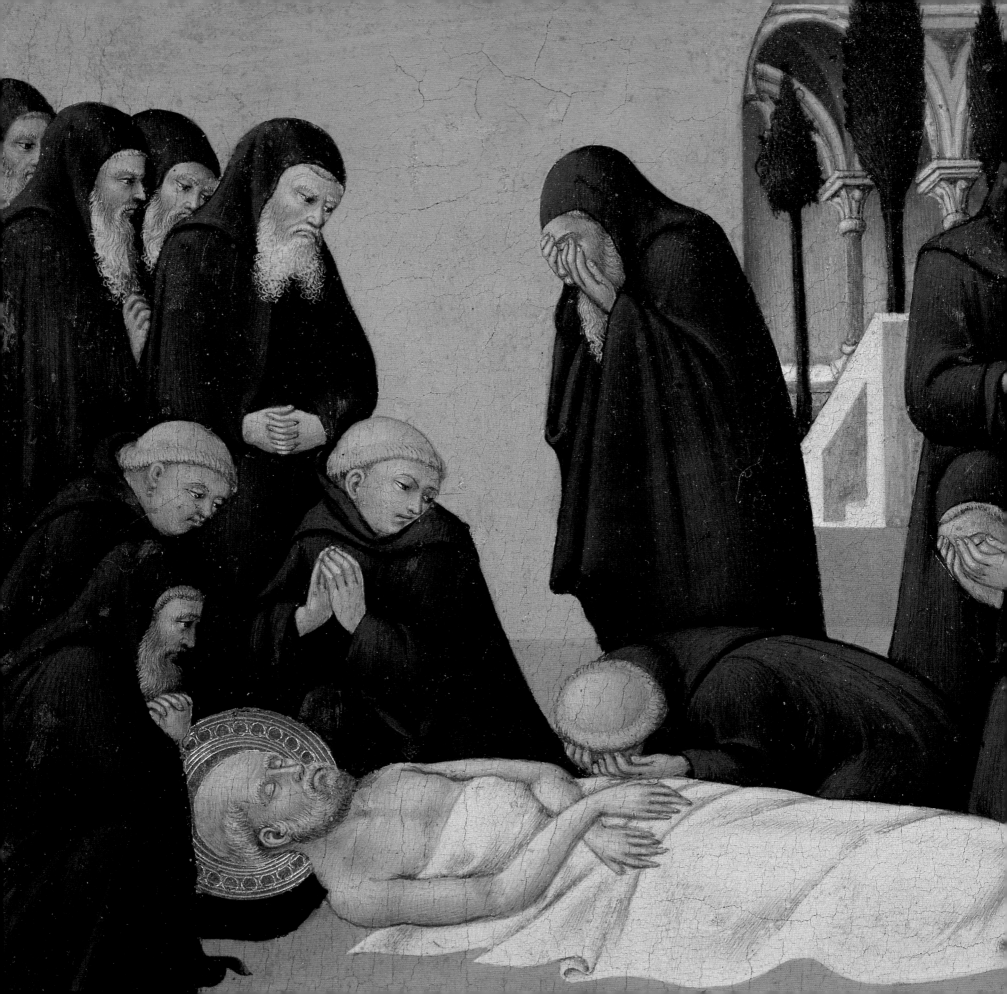

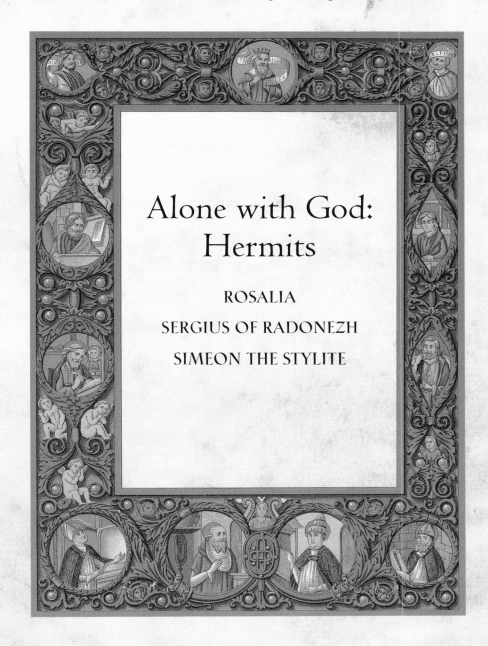

Chapter Four

Alone with God: Hermits

ROSALIA

SERGIUS OF RADONEZH

SIMEON THE STYLITE

FOLLOWING THE EXAMPLES OF JOHN THE BAPTIST (P. 91) AND CHRIST HIMSELF, BOTH OF WHOM WENT INTO THE DESERT TO FAST AND SEEK COMMUNION WITH GOD IN SOLITUDE, MANY CHRISTIANS LEFT THE TOWNS AND THE BUSINESS OF DAILY LIFE, EITHER ALONE OR IN MONASTIC COMMUNITIES, IN ORDER TO BETTER DEDICATE THEMSELVES TO GOD.

ROSALIA

SEPTEMBER 4

Rosalia was still a child when, tradition has it, she left her family to become a hermit living in a grotto near the Sicilian town of Bivona. From there she moved to Monte Pellegrino, a few miles outside Palermo, where she made her hermitage in a cave. She died there in 1160, and her body was preserved by the minerals that deposited on it.

Rosalia's first retreat, near Mount Coschina, bears on the wall the following inscription, in Latin: "I, Rosalia, daughter of

Sinibald, Lord of Quisquina, and Rosa, decided to live in this cave for the love of my Lord Jesus Christ." The Benedictines claimed the recluse as a nun, as did one of the Greek religious communities that thrived in Sicily at that time. The latter is more likely her order—the archabbey of Saint Savior in Messina formerly displayed a wooden crucifix inscribed: "I, Rosalia Sinibaldi, place this wood of my Lord, which I have ever followed, in this monastery." The cross was subsequently removed to Palermo.

In 1624, plague swept through that city. In a vision, one of the sufferers saw Rosalia; the saint directed searchers to the cave at Monte Pellegrino, where her remains were discovered, and then carried in a reliquary in procession. The plague subsided, and ever since then Rosalia has been specially venerated by the people of Palermo.

SERGIUS OF RADONEZH

SEPTEMBER 25

When the Tatars from the north rode down into Russia in the fourteenth century, they devastated everything in their path, including the monasteries—at that time and in that place, a largely urban phenomenon. The monasteries as an institution were weakened, and those individuals devoted to the spiritual life increasingly went into the wilderness.

PAGES 56 AND 57: The fifteenth-century Italian Sano di Pietro depicted the death of Jerome among his many disciples, who grieve their learned master with genuine affection, despite the irascibility for which he was famous.

LEFT: Rosalia, whom the Flemish painter Pieter Candid portrayed dressed like a fashionable society lady of the late sixteenth century, holds a rose, recalling a miracle associated with her death.

This icon of 1800 shows the Virgin with Sergius of Radonezh (second from right). The encapsulated scene above may represent one of the saint's visions.

One of the first of these hermits was Bartholomew, born in Rostov, Russia, around 1314, one of three sons of a noble family that had been forced into the peasant life at Radonezh, near Moscow, by political changes in the princi-pality. It is related that a holy man one day asked Bartholomew, the slowest of the three brothers, what he wished for. The boy answered that he wanted to be able to write, but even more to be able to read, so that he might know the Bible. After sharing the holy man's bread, which tasted sweet to him, the boy found that his wish had come true.

After the deaths of their parents, Bartholomew and his brother Stephen went to live as hermits in the forest. From the timber that grew plentifully, they erected a chapel and small house; soon after, Stephen left for a Moscow monastery. A visiting abbot gave Bartholomew the tonsure of a monk, and the new cleric took the name Sergius.

For several years, Sergius lived alone, opening his heart to nature and his soul to God. These were years of temptation and prayer, of physical hardship and grace. As his reputation for holi-ness grew, he acquired disciples. In the Russian manner, they lived in individual huts, and when there were twelve of them, Sergius accepted their request and the order of the bishop to become the abbot of the monastery of the Holy Trinity. He was ordained a priest at that time.

A town grew up around the monastery, and when the time came for the brothers to decide the direction the monastic com-munity should take, Sergius, following the advice of the patriarch at Constantinople, proposed the cenobitical, or single-residence, form. This led to dissension, including a rift with Stephen, Sergius's brother, who had returned, and Sergius left rather than even unintentionally foment discord. He founded a second hermitage but after a while returned to Holy Trinity.

The highest-ranking people in Russia, both lay and clergy, came to Sergius for counsel, including the prince of Moscow on the eve of a fateful moment in Russian history. Should the prince risk the future, even the very lives of his subjects, by resisting the Mongol Khan? With faith and fervor, Sergius urged the prince forward to his decisive, epic victory at Kulikovo Pole in 1380.

Sergius's deepest desire was for the life of the solitary, but the rest of his days were passed in traveling—always on foot, it is said—in missions of peacemaking and mediation, because that was the way of his service to his fellows and to God (though he more than once turned down invitations to be bishop of Russia). Sergius sometimes received visions, and sometimes healed the sick, and was sometimes a seer, but his cult revered his loving kindness and generosity above all. He foresaw his own death six months before it happened; he retired from his position, selected his successor, then the large, powerfully built man, who "smelled of fresh fir wood" and had never been sick, fell ill. With his spriritual brothers around him, he was given Holy Communion, and his soul passed to God in 1392.

SIMEON THE STYLITE

JANUARY 5

As a child in Cilicia (today southern Turkey, near the Syrian border), where he was born around 390, Simeon herded his father's sheep. After hearing the Beatitudes in church, and being much moved and intrigued by them, Simeon sought to learn what they meant in practical terms. The elderly man whom he consulted told the thirteen-year-old boy that con-tinual prayer, fasting, and other penances would result in the happiness promised by Christ. Throughout his life, Simeon would present a paradox, sometimes engaging in extreme physical mor-tifications of the flesh and removing himself from the world, while at the same time manifesting generosity and compassion toward his fellow human beings.

Following his conversation with the old man, Simeon haunted the gates of a nearby monastery, taking neither food nor drink for four days, and beseeching the abbot to take him in and charge him

OPPOSITE: The simple saint Sergius is memorialized in mosaic in the Church of San Marco, Venice.

ABOVE: This mosaic in the Church of San Marco in Venice may have been commissioned on the occasion of the canonization of Simeon the Stylite in 459. The ascetic saint's pillar is an elegant balustraded column with a Corinthian capital.

with the humblest tasks in the house. The abbot finally capitulated, and the boy lived in the monastery as the most menial of servants for four months, following the rigorous practices of the house, and memorizing the Psalter, which would be balm to his soul for the rest of his life. Being of a simple, open-hearted disposition, Simeon was much loved by the brothers, but after two years, he went to a second monastery, where his mortifications were so harsh that the abbot sent him away, as an example to the other monks.

Next, Simeon went to live as a hermit at Mount Telanissae, eating and drinking nothing for the forty days of Lent; he never altered this Lenten abstinence, though he was often near death at the end of the period. Three years later, Simeon moved to the top of the mountain. As time passed, the faithful began to come to him, seeking his benediction; there are records of his healing the sick in many instances. It has been said that, "despairing of escaping the world horizontally, he tried to escape it vertically": he built a platform atop a ten-foot column, and lived there for four years. ("Stylite," from the Greek, means "pillar dweller"; Simeon was the first, but not the last.)

Simeon lived for longer and longer periods on higher and higher pillars—four in all, in keeping with a vision he had had in his boyhood. The fourth and last pillar was more than sixty-six feet high. In the early years of this enterprise, the bishops and abbots of the area, concerned that Simeon's actions were expressions of self-will rather than of holy recollection, sent word that he should come down. Without a moment's hesitation, he prepared to do so; his ready obedience was all the proof the prelates required.

People thronged from every corner of the eastern Mediterranean to see Simeon, not only from the Roman Empire—Simeon's visitors included three emperors—but from the Arab lands. He converted many by the depth of his faith, the power of his virtue, and the miracles witnessed in his presence. Every afternoon, the hermit talked with those who came to him, giving commonsense counsel and sincere kindness. The patriarch of Antioch and others ministered to him, bringing him Holy Communion.

After thirty-seven years on his pillar, on July 24, 459, Simeon's soul went to God. Two days later, when his body was transported to Antioch, the move was surrounded by many miracles. A monastery and sanctuary were built at the site of Simeon's pillar; today the edifices are in ruins, but the base of the saint's last column can still be seen.

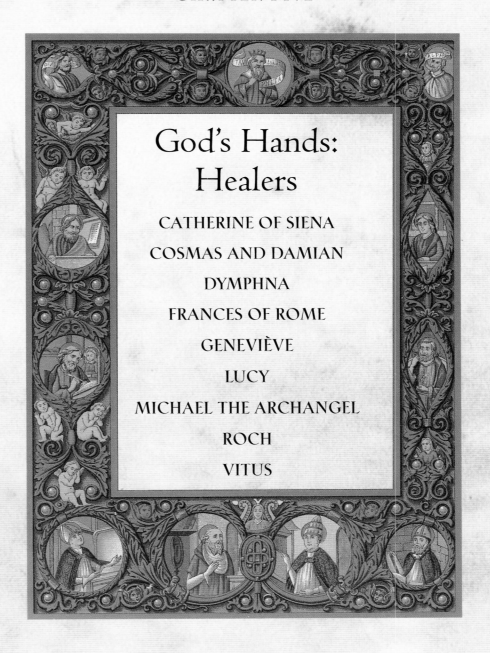

CHAPTER FIVE

God's Hands:
Healers

CATHERINE OF SIENA

COSMAS AND DAMIAN

DYMPHNA

FRANCES OF ROME

GENEVIÈVE

LUCY

MICHAEL THE ARCHANGEL

ROCH

VITUS

HEALER SAINTS BROUGHT THE BALM OF CHRISTIANITY TO AFFLICTED SOULS. WHETHER THEY LAID ON HANDS, LIKE THE PHYSICIAN BROTHERS COSMAS AND DAMIAN, OR REVIVED THE SICK WITH THEIR SPIRIT, AS THE ARCHANGEL MICHAEL DID, THEY RELIEVED THEIR FELLOWS' SUFFERING, AND FOR THAT THEY ARE VENERATED.

CATHERINE OF SIENA

APRIL 29

Caterina Benincasa's energetic and wholehearted spirituality seems to have characterized her from childhood on. Born in Siena, Italy, around 1347, the youngest of twenty-five children, she was both cheerful and deeply religious: sometimes when climbing stairs, she got down on her knees at each step to recite a Hail Mary. When she was six years old, she had a mystical vision that confirmed her early vocation: the Lord, radiant in glory between the saints Peter, Paul, and John, held out his hand to her. The enraptured Catherine could not hear her brother call her, and when at last he grabbed her hand to get her attention, the vision faded, causing Catherine to sob at the loss.

When she was twelve, approaching marriageable age, her parents urged her to dress and groom herself accordingly, and for a time she did, though she then changed her mind abruptly, announc-

PAGES 62 AND 63: The German painter Julius Schnorr von Carolsfeld portrays an aristocratic Roch distributing alms. The artist found a way to insert the dog that is one of the saint's most enduring—and endearing—emblems.

OPPOSITE: This anonymous fifteenth-century painting of Catherine of Siena was done as an ex-voto, that is, in gratitude to the saint for a successful intercession.

ing that she would not marry. Her parents continued to look for a husband for her, until Catherine attempted to put an end to the discussion by cutting off her long, rich hair. Angrily, her father and mother began a campaign to break the girl's will, assigning her the most humble chores, refusing her the comfort of privacy that she so cherished, and scolding her constantly. She later wrote in her great mystical work, *The Dialogue*, that she had learned from God during that period to find a refuge within herself that could remain always untouched and serene. Her father at last relented, and Catherine was once again granted her solitude—a small, dimly lit room, in which she lived ascetically. When, at about twenty years old, she became a Dominican tertiary, that is, a lay sister living in the world but following some part of the Dominican rule, she increased her physical mortifications, punishing her flesh to purify her soul.

She continued to receive heavenly visions, but she was also beset by hideous sights and grotesque, seductive temptations. Worst of all were the times when she felt that God had abandoned her to these nightmare trials: "Oh Lord," she prayed, "where wert Thou when my heart was so sorely vexed with foul and hateful temptations?" Came the reply: "Daughter, I was in thy heart, fortifying thee by my grace." Finally, she received a vision in which she was spiritually wed to Christ, and shortly after was called to work in the world.

At first, Catherine nursed the sick, including lepers and others suffering from disfiguring diseases. Until her death, she would be the object of both loving praise and malicious rumors of fanaticism and hypocrisy—this despite the number of witnesses who saw Catherine rise inches off the ground when in

prayer. Little by little, she attracted around her a spiritual family of every class and condition, who called her "Mamma."

During an outbreak of the plague, Catherine and her spiritual family nursed and comforted the afflicted; she also visited many who were condemned to death, bringing them the hope of salvation. She went joyfully through her life and was a moving and effective advocate who returned many souls to God. Her down-to-earth holiness inspired her neighbors and others to consult her, and she was often called upon to act as mediator in all kinds of disputes.

In 1375, in Pisa, Catherine attended Mass, took Holy Communion, and was meditating on the crucified Christ, when she received the stigmata so painfully that she fainted. The five wounds—in hands, feet, and side, like those Christ received on the cross—remained invisible to others during her lifetime. Little more than a year later, Catherine was at Avignon, in France, following up her correspondence with Pope Gregory XI concerning the return of the papacy, after almost seventy-five years, from Avignon to Rome. (It is reported that upon meeting with the pontiff, Catherine said to him, "Fulfill what you have promised," though he had never mentioned his vow that he would return to Rome to any person.) Gregory XI did indeed return to the Holy City but died shortly after, in 1378.

The new pope, Urban VI, was elected and almost immediately began a policy of centralizing power in the hands of the pope, countering the trend of Avignon, which had endowed the College of Cardinals with great authority. Besides displaying a personal and impolitic authoritarianism, Urban VI exhibited clear signs of mental instability. Claiming that his election had been forced upon them by the Roman populace, the College of Cardinals elected the "antipope" Clement VII and, with him, returned to Avignon.

This schism, or split, was tearing Europe in two, with nations taking sides and even parishes rent between Urbanist and Clementine priests. Each of the popes excommunicated the supporters of the other, and Christendom in the West was in spiritual and political chaos. Catherine threw herself into the breach, supporting Urban as the legitimate head of the Church (but not

OPPOSITE: Under the eyes of the Virgin and Child, Cosmas and Damian perform a miracle of healing, in a fifteenth-century painting by the Spanish artist Fernando del Rincòn.

neglecting to reprove him for a tyrannical manner that was driving away even those who endorsed his cause). The indefatigable Catherine dictated hundreds, perhaps thousands of letters, some four hundred of which survive, illustrating the candor, even brusqueness and familiarity, for which she is renowned.

Urban VI called Catherine to Rome on several occasions, and it was there that she died following a stroke, worn out at only thirty-three years of age by years of relentless physical pain. In 1970, she, with Teresa of Ávila, was declared a Doctor of the Church.

COSMAS AND DAMIAN

SEPTEMBER 26

Cosmas and Damian were twins, two of five sons born in the third century to a pious woman named Theodoche in Syria. The twins were both physicians, "endowed by the Holy Ghost with such grace that they healed all ills of man and beasts." They never charged for their services, believing that as Christians they should own nothing. One day a woman who had spent all her fortune on doctors with no result came to them. Damian cured her, and she offered him a small sum in gratitude, asking him to accept in the name of the Lord. For this reason, and for courtesy's sake, Damian accepted, but in a fit of righteousness Cosmas ordered that, when the time came, Damian was not to be buried with him. That night, in a dream, the Lord told Cosmas that Damian was not guilty.

The persecutions of the Roman emperor Diocletian were sweeping the provinces, and Lisias, the proconsul of Syria, hearing of Cosmas and Damian, summoned them along with their brothers and ordered them all to bow down before the pagan gods. This they refused to do. Lisias ordered them tortured and thrown into the sea, but the brothers, aided by angels, remained staunch.

Believing them to be powerful magicians, the proconsul invited the Christians to teach him their arts, whereupon two demons appeared and hit him. Lisias took this as a sign of the pagan gods' displeasure and redoubled his torments of the Christian brothers. He commanded that they be stoned, but the stones turned back upon those who hurled them; when the proconsul ordered archers to shoot the brothers, many of

the archers were themselves wounded when their arrows flew back at them.

Finally, Lisias, in a fury, gave the order for the brothers to be beheaded at dawn. Their fellow Christians remembered Cosmas's injunction to bury them separately, but a camel approached them and told them to bury the twins together. Even after their death, Cosmas and Damian, the patron saints of doctors, performed miracles of healing, often for the faithful who slept in their churches, including a peasant who had swallowed a snake as he slept, and a man with a cancerous leg.

DYMPHNA
MAY 15

In the thirteenth century, two marble coffins were unearthed in Geel, Belgium. They contained the bones of a woman and a man; a nearby brick bore the inscription DYMPNA, and soon a tale arose that transformed the remains into holy relics. Dymphna (sometimes confused with the Irish Saint Damhnait) was a Celtic beauty in the seventh century—Irish, perhaps, or British, or Armorican—born to a Christian princess and a pagan king.

Dymphna received instruction in the Christian faith and was baptized while still a little girl; shortly after, her mother died, leaving her father inconsolable, even obsessed. When Dymphna became a young woman, she came to look so like her mother that her father, thinking only of his late wife, made incestuous advances toward his daughter. Dymphna's confessor, Saint Gerebernus, advised the girl to leave home and together they set sail for Antwerp, along with the court jester and his wife, who were also Christians.

They landed in Antwerp, then traveled through the woods, stopping finally some twenty-five miles away, at a small chapel in honor of Saint Martin, where the town of Geel stands today. Dymphna and her companions decided to live there as hermits, but the king, her father, had set spies after them and found them. When Dymphna continued to resist him, her father commanded his soldiers to cut off the Christians' heads. The henchmen killed Gerebernus, but were reluctant to murder the princess. Enraged, the king beheaded his daughter himself. The pagans abandoned the bodies to the creatures of the forest, but angels—or merciful Christians—buried them.

In the thirteenth century, numerous instances of people cured of epilepsy or madness after approaching her relics made Dymphna the patron saint of those so afflicted. By the end of that century, a hospital was founded for the treatment of the mentally ill; it still exists and is a model of its kind.

FRANCES OF ROME
MARCH 9

Francesca Busso, born in Rome in 1384, was the daughter of noble, religious, and doting parents, Paolo Busso and Giacobella dei Roffredeschi. Frances was only eleven, but already deeply aware of her vocation, when she asked her parents' permission to become a nun. To her surprise and dismay, her parents said no, some months later telling her that she was engaged to be married to an excellent young man, Lorenzo de' Ponziani. In time, Frances agreed to the marriage, and the nuptials took place when she was thirteen. Frances and Lorenzo were harmoniously married for forty years, with never a word of unkindness nor a quarrel between them.

Throughout her life, Frances cherished the spiritual nature of everyday tasks—as she once said of homemakers like herself, "Sometimes she must leave God at the altar to find Him in her housekeeping." When her mother-in-law died, the family asked Frances to take the older woman's place in governing the household palace, Palazzo Ponziano, though her husband was not the elder son. Out of obedience, she agreed. Her legend has it that one day she was at her prayers when her husband called for her; she went imediately, then returned to her reading and meditation. This happened three more times, until, returning to her meditations, she opened her book once more, to find the verse she had been reading written in gold.

Together with her sister-in-law, Frances cared for the sick and suffering in those years of plague and war. She was criticized by some for not taking more of a part in the worldly pleasures considered proper to her rank, but Lorenzo firmly seconded her in all she did. As time went on, she was beset by temptations, hideous yet compelling apparitions that threatened to engulf her, but she prayed and went about her duties with care and gentleness.

The schism between the supporters of Pope Gregory XII and the faction for Benedict XIII, the "antipope" in Avignon, turned violent. In 1409, Palazzo Ponziano was ransacked and robbed, and Lorenzo was forced to abandon his home and flee Rome. In his absence, Frances lost a son to an epidemic, and poor as she now was, she turned part of her home into a hospital. Miracles of healing began soon after. In 1414, Lorenzo returned, shattered by his experiences. Their wealth was restored, but not before their daughter, too, had died.

All Rome knew of Frances, and many came calling on her as a healer and peacemaker. Lorenzo, more in love with her than ever, released her from her wifely obligations on condition that she continue to live in their home with him. Freed of domestic concerns, Frances gathered together a number of ladies of the aristocracy who felt as she did; they were not bound by vows—though they were affiliated with a Benedictine house—but only dedicated to God and to the poor. They came to be known as the Oblates of Tor de' Specchi, when they bought a house of that name seven years later.

After Lorenzo passed away in 1436, Frances asked to be admitted to Tor de' Specchi as an oblate, a layperson who lives in a convent or monastery, and was joyfully received. In her final years, she moved even closer to her God, experiencing more and more visions and ecstasies. Since the death of her daughter, Frances had seen an archangel accompanying her. In 1440, at the hour of Frances's death, her face glowed, as she said, "The angel has finished his task; he beckons me to follow him."

People crowded into her home, some carrying their sick and dying in hopes of healing. Her body was taken to the church now known by her name, where the miracles of healing multiplied. Frances's foundation still lives, and fervent pilgrims still visit Palazzo Ponziano during the week of her feast day.

GEΠEVIÈVE

JANUARY 3

Saint Germanus, bishop of Auxerre, was on his way to Britain in 429, when he stopped in Nanterre, then a small town outside of Paris, today a suburb. The people of the town sought his blessing, and among them he noticed a little girl about nine years old. Germanus asked to speak to her

parents, and when he met Severus and Gerontia, he prophesied that their daughter, the little shepherdess Geneviève (Genovefa), would be a saint. He then ascertained from the child herself her fond wish to serve God.

Geneviève's wish came true when she was fifteen; with two other girls, she received the veil that marked her as a dedicated virgin. She fasted sometimes five days a week, and, when she did eat, on Sundays and Thursdays, her meals were modest—"barley bread and beans."

When her parents died, her godmother in Paris took the young woman in. Although Geneviève lived a life of prayer, charity, and pilgrimages, and continued to be supported by Germanus and loved by many, she also had enemies, perhaps due at least in part to her gift for prophesy. (She is sometimes depicted in art holding a candle whose flame is contested by an angel and a devil.)

During the terrifying, seemingly inexorable advance of Attila and the conquering Huns of the fifth century, the people's mistrust of Geneviève flared into panicked attacks on her. Germanus's archdeacon calmed the populace, and endorsed Geneviève's courageous advice to stay in the city. Attila unaccountably veered away from Paris, toward Orléans, and the Parisians instantly changed their attitude toward the young woman, fervently believing a miracle to have occurred in answer to Geneviève's prayers.

The next invaders were the Franks, who blockaded the city. Geneviève led a troop of desperate citizens up the Seine to procure food for the resisting Parisians, and although the Franks' leader, Childeric, a pagan, took Paris, he followed Geneviève's counsel and showed much mercy during the occupation. His son, Clovis, converted to Christianity by his wife, Saint Clotilda, similarly allowed himself to be led to mercy by the brave and pious Geneviève.

She is the patron saint of Paris, not only because of her courageous defense of the city and its people during her lifetime, but for her care for them after her death, which took place around 500. One of the most notable instances of Genieviève's intercession, which is still celebrated annually, was the sudden cessation—more than six centuries after her death—of a violent outbreak of ergotism, an illness bringing madness and death. Follwoing fervent prayers and a procession with her relics, the suffering were miraculously restored to health.

LUCY
DECEMBER 13

Lucy, a pious early-fourth-century maiden of Syracuse, Sicily, and a loving daughter, accompanied her mother to the tomb of Agatha (p. 48) so that her mother might be cured of a hemorrhage. As they prayed, Lucy fell asleep and had a vision in which Agatha addressed her as "sister" and "virgin consecrated to God," even though Lucy was betrothed. Saint Agatha also asked Lucy why she was praying to her for a cure that Lucy's own prayers could effect. Lucy awoke, told her mother that

ABOVE: Lucy, dressed in a Renaissance notion of Roman robes, holds the palm of martyrdom in her left hand. Today she is still invoked in cases of eye trouble.

OPPOSITE: The fifteenth-century Felmish painter Rogier van der Weyden shows Michael as the weigher of souls.

she was healed, and asked her to release her from her engagement. Her mother agreed, and, together, mother and daughter began to sell what they owned in order to give all to the poor.

Lucy's greedy fiancé wanted to know why the two ladies were selling their property; when he learned that they were giving everything to the poor, he denounced Lucy as a Christian. The Roman consul, Paschasius, invited Lucy to sacrifice to the pagan idols, but the spirited girl refused. They argued, until finally Paschasius challenged Lucy to say whether she had the Holy Ghost within. Lucy replied, "Whosoever lives chastely is the temple of the Holy Ghost," whereupon Paschasius threatened to commit her to a brothel. Undaunted, Lucy countered, "The body is not soiled unless the soul consents; and if in my despite my body is ravished, my chastity will thereby be doubled."

Paschasius went to act on his threat and called together the panders (pimps, madams, and the ilk) of the city to carry Lucy off, but she was suddenly so heavy that no number of men or oxen could move her. Magicians were summoned, but they, too, were useless. Then the consul, in a fury, commanded that boiling substances be poured over Lucy, but she only answered, "God has granted that I should bear these delays in my martyrdom, in order to free the faithful from the fear of suffering, and to take away from unbelievers any reason for denying His power."

In an uncontainable rage, the consul had Lucy stabbed in the throat with a sword. She continued to speak, announcing that Maximian was dead and Diocletian deposed; at that moment, messengers from the new emperor arrived to arrest Paschasius. Lucy waited to die until she had received Holy Communion; she was buried on the place of her martyrdom, and later a church was built there.

Perhaps because her name means "light," she is the patron saint of eyesight and is shown holding a plate with one or two eyes on it.

MICHAEL THE ARCHANGEL
SEPTEMBER 29

As often as there is a work of wondrous power to be wrought, Michael is sent to perform it." This mighty angel is an important figure in both the Old and the New Testaments, and in both the Eastern Church, where he is

protector of the sick, and the Western, where he is the patron saint of all Christians, and of soldiers. (Another patron saint of soldiers is Joan of Arc [p. 88]; Michael was one of her voices.) Michael has fought the Devil and his demons since he triumphed over them and cast them out of Heaven; it is he who welcomes the holy souls to Paradise; and it is his voice who will call the dead to rise again. Michael, it is said, has often appeared on earth, but three of his visits are especially well known.

In the late fifth century, Michael appeared on Mount Gargano in southeastern Italy, announcing that he wished to make that place his earthly home. When his church was built and consecrated, he placed his mantle upon the altar: the angel's feast day, also known as Michaelmas, commemorates the consecration of the church.

A second apparition took place in northwest France. There, too, Michael had a church built on a hill, a rock surrounded by water, today still named for the archangel: Mont-Saint-Michel. When the church was consecrated, Michael brought a piece of his cloak from Mount Gargano, along with a fragment of the marble on which he had stood.

The third apparition was vouchsafed to Pope Saint Gregory the Great. During a terrible plague in Rome, Gregory was praying that the people be delivered, when he saw above the mausoleum of the emperor Hadrian the radiant archangel Michael drying blood off his sword, then sheathing it, a heavenly sign that the plague was over. In gratitude, Gregory had a church built on the site, today known as Castel Sant'Angelo—the Fortress of the Holy Angel.

In the twentieth century, the archangels Gabriel and Raphael, once venerated by the Eastern Church but only locally in western Europe, joined Michael in being honored on his day.

ROCH
AUGUST 16

His cult was immediate, fervent, and enduring—today, as Roch in France and Rocco in Italy, this beloved saint is still invoked against illness, and there is evidence that his cult extended as far as the British Isles at one time. Little is known about him, except that he was born in the fourteenth century, probably in Montpellier, France, a son of the governor of that city.

Orphaned at twenty, Roch left home to go on pilgrimage to Rome, only to find the plague sweeping through northern

OPPOSITE: The Neapolitan artist Luca Giordano vividly portrayed the moral dimension of Satan's (temporary) defeat at the hands of the archangel Michael.

ABOVE: The Venetian artist Carlo Crivelli painted the beloved Roch, identifiable by his pilgrim's staff and broad-brimmed hat. He points to the inflammation typical of the plague, of which he was miraculously cured.

Italy. The Franciscans claim him as a tertiary of their order, that is, a lay person who observes part of the Franciscan rule, and it may have been in that capacity that he turned to nursing the sick. The young Frenchman traveled throughout the plague-stricken cities of northern Italy, caring for the suffering and dying, and in some cases effecting cures when he made the sign of the cross over the patient. At Piacenza, he exhibited symptoms himself, and went off to die alone in the forest; a dog came to him, fed him for a time, then led his master to the dying healer. The man took Roch to his home and tended him until he recovered completely.

According to legend, Roch's powers to heal became greater after his illness, and in Piacenza he cured many people and their cattle as well. He made his way back to Montpellier, where he was accused of being an impostor and imprisoned; he died in jail around 1378. There is another tradition that holds that Roch was arrested as a spy in Lombardy and died in prison there. Numerous miracles have been credited to Roch's intercession since his death.

VITUS

JUNE 15

The cult of Vitus, or Vito, is ancient in Italy and Germany; he is particularly invoked against epilepsy; "Saint Vitus's dance," that is, chorea, a nervous disorder affecting human beings and dogs; and mad dogs; he is also the patron saint of comedians and dancers. Little of his history is known except that he was probably from Lucania, in southern Italy, and suffered martyrdom in the third century during the reign of the Roman emperors Diocletian and Maximian.

According to Vitus's legend, his father, a pagan, used to thrash his son for showing disdain for the gods, and Vitus was no more than twelve when the prefect Valerianus came to know of the young Christian's resistance. The prefect had Vitus brought before him and challenged him to sacrifice to the idols; Vitus refused, and the prefect gestured to have him beaten. But even as Vitus's torturers raised their arms to strike, they felt their strength suddenly drain and their limbs wither. The prefect, too, stared at his own mysteriously withered hand. Vitus prayed, and instantly his tormentors' arms and the prefect's hand were made

whole. Valerianus ordered Vitus's father to take the boy home, "Lest some evil death befall him!"

In an attempt to distract his son from his piety, Vitus's father brought musicians and dancing girls into the house; other times, he locked Vitus in his room. Once, when Vitus was shut in, there was a heavenly scent throughout the house; when his father went to investigate, seven angels surrounded the little prisoner, and at the sight Vitus's father was struck blind. He went to the temple of Jupiter, where he vowed to sacrifice a bull with gilt horns if the god would heal him, but it was in vain. Vitus offered up a prayer, and his father was able to see once more.

Vitus's father, angrier than ever, determined to put his son to death himself, but before he could carry out his vow, an angel appeared to Modestus, Vitus's tutor and the husband of the boy's nurse, Crescentia, and told him to take the boy away by sea. Modestus obeyed the heavenly command, and the three were miraculously fed by an eagle until they landed.

Meanwhile, the son of the emperor Diocletian was possessed, the demon that inhabited him swearing that he would leave only if Vitus came. The emperor had Vitus brought to court, and there, through Vitus's intercession, God cast the demon out. But Diocletian was prisoner of his own edict decreeing death to the Christians, and he begged Vitus to sacrifice to the idols, or perish. Vitus refused and was imprisoned along with his two companions. In their cell, the shackles dropped from them, while the air around them was filled with a celestial radiance.

Next, the emperor had the three thrust into a red-hot furnace, but they remained unscathed. A starving lion, sent to devour them, was tamed by their joyous trust in God and rolled at their feet like a kitten. Then, just as Vitus and his companions were being fastened to the rack, a thundering earthquake brought the temples down on the pagans within and sent the idols crashing to the ground. Diocletian, bewailing his defeat by a child, escaped the devastation.

The three Christians found themselves transported to the banks of a cool, flowing river, where they prayed together before giving their souls up to God.

OPPOSITE: Angelically blond and clad in princely garments, as befitting a member of the nobility of the saints, the young Vitus's simple and certain faith is evident in his serene and joyous gaze.

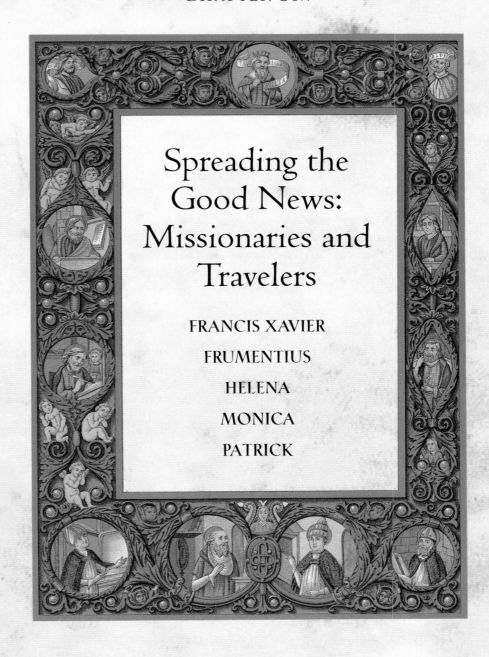

CHAPTER SIX

Spreading the Good News: Missionaries and Travelers

FRANCIS XAVIER

FRUMENTIUS

HELENA

MONICA

PATRICK

HELENA
AUGUST 18

Her parents, of modest station, were perhaps innkeepers in Drepanum—which her affectionate and respectful son would later rename Helenopolis—in northern Asia Minor, where Helena was born around 248. It may have been at her family's inn that the Roman general Constantius Chlorus ("the Pale") met and married Helena around the year 270. An ambitious soldier, he was irresistibly drawn to this young woman of character as well as beauty.

In 274, their son, Constantine, was born in Naissus, in present-day Serbia, and in 293, Constantius was made caesar. He succumbed to political pressure to leave Helena to marry the daughter of the emperor Maximian, who with Diocletian would so savagely persecute the Christians (and whom Constantine would have executed after himself ascending the imperial throne).

When Constantine became emperor in 306, he raised his mother to the highest ranks, inventing a title in her honor: *nobilissima femina*, "noblest of women." In 312, according to tradition, Constantine saw a vision of a cross accompanied by the words *in hoc signo vinces*: "You will be victorious by this sign." Both Constantine and Helena may have converted at that time, or somewhat earlier; Helena was in her early sixties, and her new life was just beginning.

Mother and son were both vigorously active Christians. In 313, Constantine promulgated the Edict of Milan, extending religious tolerance to the Christians, and, in his efforts to heal ecclesiastical schisms and to suppress heresies such as Arianism (which denied that Father and Son are of the same substance), he was instrumental in shaping the early church. Where earlier rulers had spent the vast resources of the imperial treasury in pleasure and politics, Helena used them to mitigate the misery of the poor of the empire and to build churches. In her mid-seventies, she made a pilgrimage to Jerusalem, where she founded the churches of the Nativity and of the Holy Sepulcher.

LEFT: Helena holds the True Cross, too holy to touch with bare fingers, and the golden nails in this early-fifteenth-century Spanish painting. The three nails and three sets of three pleats may refer to the Holy Trinity.

To build the latter, Helena razed a temple of Venus that had been built on Calvary; her legend relates that she found the Holy Cross there by ruthlessly interrogating Judas, a Jewish man who had learned the secret of where the Holy Cross was from his dying father. The place revealed its nature with the rich scent of spices, which is often associated with holiness, and Judas was instantly converted. Three crosses were found at the site, and each one was tested, until the third cross brought a dead man back to life.

Judas was baptized, taking the name Cyriacus. He was ordained a bishop, and Helena asked him to find the three nails with which Christ was crucified. Cyriacus returned to Calvary and prayed there until the nails, as radiant as gold, revealed themselves, whereupon Helena took them and gave two to her son. Constantine set one of the nails into his warhorse's bridle and the other into his statue on a hill above Rome. Helena threw the third nail into the Adriatic Sea to calm an ancient whirlpool that had taken the lives of numberless sailors. She decreed that the day of the finding of the Cross should be commemorated; the feast day is May 3. Helena is the patron saint of archaeologists. She died in Nicomedia around 330.

MONICA
AUGUST 27

Monica and her history are known from the writings of her son Augustine (p. 112). She was born in Tagaste, Numidia, around the year 331. A devout Christian, she was sorrowed by her brilliant son's worldly ambitions, contempt for her religion, and long-standing sexual relationship with a woman he did not marry. In her anguish, Monica sought counsel from a bishop, who comforted her with a near-prophecy: "It is not possible that a son of so many tears should be lost."

Monica braved the hazards of travel to follow Augustine to Rome, then to Milan, where she joined the followers of Saint Ambrose, the bishop of that city who had so impressed Augustine. When Augustine at last was baptized, the joyful Monica was one of those who joined him on his subsequent retreat.

Mother and son set out to return together to Africa, and at Ostia, the port of Rome, they shared grateful, loving conversa-

tions on the wonders of salvation while they awaited their ship. But Monica suddenly fell ill, and in only a matter of days she died in Ostia in the year 387.

PATRICK
MARCH 17

Patricius was a Romanized Briton, born on the west coast of what is today England, near Wales, around 385. His family was Christian: his father, Calpurnius, was a deacon as well as a government administrator, and Patricius's grandfather had been a priest (this was before priests were celibate). Patricius, however, as he wrote in his *Confession*, was not very religious, and he held priests in low regard.

At sixteen, he was kidnapped by raiders and sold into slavery in Ireland, where he tended flocks for a local warlord—throughout his long life, he would speak out against slavery. In absolute solitude, always hungry and often cold, the boy began to pray constantly. "The love of God . . . grew in me more and more, as did the faith," he wrote, "and my soul was rosed, so that, in a single day, I have said as many as a hundred prayers, and in the night, nearly the same." His prayers brought him to an all-embracing sense of God—"the Creator of Creation"—and one night he received a vision inviting him to escape. As he had been instructed in his vision, he fled to the coast, where he found a ship waiting. After a series of wonders, he arrived home once more.

Again, his voices spoke, this time directing him to go study at the island monastery at

OPPOSITE: Monica, mother of Augustine, prays for the conversion of her pagan son in this fresco of 1463–65 by Benozzo Gozzoli. In a second episode, she blesses her young son, unaware of his glorious future.

RIGHT: This miniature of Patrick before the high king of Ireland is from a manuscript of The Golden Legend, *a source of many of the sermons delivered on the saints' days of the religious calendar.*

Lérins, in the south of France, across from Cannes. This he did, although he had had only a few years' education before his visions instructed him to return to Ireland: in a dream, he heard the "voice of the Irish", who called out, "We beg you, holy youth, to come and walk among us once more." He became a bishop, the most successful of the many missionaries who worked to convert Ireland to Christianity in the fifth century. Patrick is not one of the scholar saints—in fact, he was often accused of "rusticity," or a lack of a higher education. But his vast love and deep concern for the individuals in his spiritual care echo across the centuries in his writings, including his *Confession*, an explanation of his life and his conduct. He died in Saul, Down, Ireland, in 461.

Patrick was not the first missionary to bring Christianity to Ireland, but he found a way to help Ireland take Christianity to its ancient heart. He is sometimes shown with snakes, which he is said to have banished from Ireland, or with a shamrock, which he is said to have used to illustrate the doctrine of the Trinity.

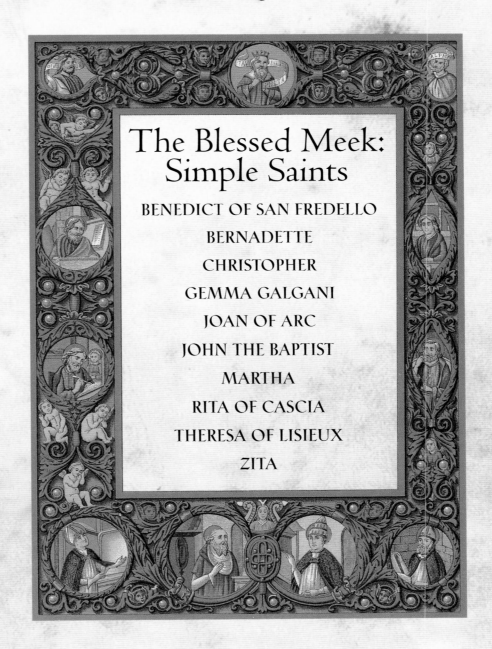

CHAPTER SEVEN

The Blessed Meek: Simple Saints

BENEDICT OF SAN FREDELLO

BERNADETTE

CHRISTOPHER

GEMMA GALGANI

JOAN OF ARC

JOHN THE BAPTIST

MARTHA

RITA OF CASCIA

THERESA OF LISIEUX

ZITA

THE SIMPLEST PERSON CAN BECOME A SAINT BY SERVING GOD WITH DEVOTION. SOMETIMES LIVING A HUMBLE, MODEST LIFE IS THE MOST HOLY THING ONE CAN DO. WHILE SOME OF THESE SAINTS' DEEDS, SUCH AS THOSE OF JOAN OF ARC, WERE NOT ALWAYS SIMPLE, THE PIETY THAT DROVE THEM TO SUCH ACTIONS WAS OF THE MOST ELEMENTAL KIND.

BENEDICT OF SAN FREDELLO

APRIL 4

Benedict Manasseri was deeply religious from his youngest days, and his piety, combined with a remarkably good nature, earned him the nickname *il moro santo* (the black saint) by which he would be known all his life. Born in 1526, he was the eldest son of devout Christian parents, Nubian slaves of a man of property near Messina, Sicily, who kept his promise to Christopher, Benedict's father, that he would free his son.

One day, when Benedict was about twenty-one, a group of Franciscan hermits passing through the neighborhood were stopped by the crudity of certain insults addressed to a modest young man. The hermits were even more struck by the dignity and gentleness of Benedict's reply, and their leader, named Lanzi, prophesied to the young man's tormentors that "you will hear great things of him." Then, on the spot, he asked Benedict to join their group; Benedict accepted.

PAGES 84 AND 85: Christopher's size dwarfs the trees, and he walks thigh-deep in water as the Child's weight miraculously increases. The medieval devout believed that whoever looked at an image of Saint Christopher would be safe for that day.

The community moved more than once; their last home was at Monte Pellegrino, where Rosalia (p. 58) had died. There, Lanzi breathed his last, and Benedict, much against his inclination, was elected the community's superior. In simple obedience, he only sought to do good in every circumstance, and in all humility, without excessive penances or harsh mortifications, though he never ceased the practices he had adopted as a hermit. He used to say that it was better to eat only a little, then stop, than to deprive oneself of food altogether.

About 1564, the community of hermits dispersed, and Benedict was accepted as a lay brother of the Friars Minor—the Franciscans—of the Observance in a monastery near Palermo. A shy person, he worked with great satisfaction in the kitchen, but the power of his goodness was soon discovered. A phenomenon exhibited by certain saints, his face shone with a holy light when he was hearing Mass. Miracles began to occur, such as the multiplication of food in his hands. He also became a famous healer.

Some fourteen years later, Benedict's order determined that the monastery in which he lived would become a house of the reform, that is, governed by a stricter observance of the rule of Francis (p. 102) than previously. Once again, Benedict, though a lay brother, was chosen as the superior of the community, this time during the tumultuous period of adjustment to the new rule. Though he was illiterate, Benedict's profound understanding of theological issues, his intellectual clarity, his patience, and his tact endowed him with an authority that enabled him to lead his brothers in a recommitment to Francis's spiritual values.

Benedict filled other positions as well, but after a time he was permitted to return to the kitchens, where he received all who came to him, whether for his counsel, for alms, or for his healing powers. The visitors were of every station, and to all he extended his compassion. He died in 1589. Known as Benedict the Moor, he is the patron saint of African-Americans.

BERNADETTE
APRIL 16

Marie Bernarde Soubirous was the sickly eldest child of thriftless millers, Francis Soubirous and Louise Casterot, the latter not yet out of her teens when her first child was born in 1844, in Lourdes, France. The neighbors were fond of Bernadette, who was a remarkably amiable child, somewhat small for her age, and slow but kind and gifted with great common sense.

On February 11, 1858, about a month after she turned fourteen, Bernadette saw, in a grotto on the banks of the Gave, a very young, very lovely Lady, who talked sweetly to her of prayer and penitence. People began to join Bernadette at her visits to the grotto, and by March 4 their numbers had reached 200,000, though no one but Bernadette saw the Lady, who told the girl to have a shrine erected there. The Lady showed Bernadette where to dig, and in that spot a spring appeared; the Lady said that pilgrims to the shrine could bathe in the waters of that spring and drink from them. On March 25, the Lady identifed herself, in the dialect of the region, saying, "I am the Immaculate Conception."

Bernadette last saw the Lady on July 16, the Feast of Our Lady of Mount Carmel, which commemorates an appearance by the Virgin at Mount Carmel, but Bernadette's own trials were just beginning. Assailed by believers and unbelievers alike, the girl could find no tranquility, though she maintained her even temper and patience, as she had done throughout the five months of her visions. In 1866, she entered the convent of the Sisters of Charity in Nevers, hundreds of miles from her home and the site of her visions with the Lady. Her health was uneven, and it gradually worsened, though she was able to be of service to the convent. She

died in 1879, at thirty-five years old. She was canonized in 1933, not for her visions but for her lifelong simple faith and humility. Her official name in the Church rolls is Saint Mary Bernarda.

CHRISTOPHER
JULY 25

Reprobus, his name meaning "outcast," was a Canaanite giant, some twenty feet tall and frightening of aspect. He served the king of Canaan, but the desire came to him to serve the mightiest ruler there was. Having often heard a particular king thus described, Reprobus went to find him and entered his service.

At that king's court, a musician sang a song that spoke of the Devil; every time the mighty king heard the Devil mentioned, he made the sign of the cross. From this, Reprobus concluded that, since the king feared the Devil, the Devil was more powerful than the king. Accordingly, Reprobus went in search of the Devil and found him—"a soldier fierce and terrible of visage"—at the head of an army. Reprobus joined the Devil's army, but when they came to a crossroads and to a cross that stood there he saw the Devil flinch, and so he understood that Christ was stronger still.

Determined to serve Christ, Reprobus went to a hermit for instruction. The hermit told him to fast, but Reprobus said he could not. The hermit told him to pray, but Reprobus said he

Hans Memling haloed the Blessing Child in swirling drapery that contrasts with Christopher's dark, gravity-prone robes and emphasizes the wonder of the event.

could not do that, either. Finally, the hermit told him to go build himself a hut by a certain rushing river, where he was to help people to the other side. This Reprobus could do. One night, the giant was awakened by a child asking to be taken across the rushing river. Reprobus took his great staff and hoisted the child on his great shoulders, but at midstream the waters rose and the child became so heavy that Reprobus almost failed to reach the far bank.

On dry land once more, Reprobus marveled, exclaiming that it was as if he had carried the whole world. The child answered him: "Wonder not, Christopher, for not only hast thou borne the whole world upon thy shoulders, but Him who created the world!" And so Reprobus took the name Christopher, which means "bearer of Christ."

GEMMA GALGANI

APRIL 11

Gemma Galgani was born to a wealthy family in Camigliano, Italy, in 1878. When her family's fortunes declined, Gemma, then about nineteen years old, went to work as a servant for a family in Lucca. Her health was never good, and she suffered physically all her life, in particular from curvature of the spine due to tuberculosis. Gemma was especially devoted to Saint Gabriel Possenti (1838–1862), also known as Saint Gabriel of Our Lady of Sorrows, who belonged to the Passionist Order and was himself consumptive. Following an apparition of this simple, cheerful saint, Gemma experienced a complete cure of her spinal condition. More cautious doctors, however, refused to give her the medical certificate of good health that she required to enter the Passionist Order herself.

Gemma was profoundly serene by nature, radiating charity and love. She prayed continually, living in almost constant communion with God; for a year and a half in her early twenties, she sometimes displayed the stigmata, or marks of Christ's crucifixion, as well as, later, the welts of his scourging. She frequently experienced ecstasies, in which she spoke aloud to her visions, and many of Gemma's utterances were recorded. On the other hand, she was at times violently possessed by demonic forces, spitting on the crucifix and one time tearing a rosary apart.

Throughout her life, Gemma bore all with fortitude, good nature, and faith, including her last, protracted illness. She died in peace at twenty-five, in Lucca, Italy, in 1903, and still enjoys a popular cult.

JOAN OF ARC

MAY 30

Jeanne la Pucelle, or Joan the Maid, born on the feast day of the Epiphany in Domrémy, France, around 1412, was the daughter of farmers in the Champagne region of France. She was proud of her skill at sewing and spinning, and neighbors remembered her as generous, pious, kind, and well loved. Civil war was raging throughout France, and the town of Domrémy was particularly vulnerable; at least once the d'Arc family had to take refuge in nearby Neufchâteau from plundering Burgundians. Much of France was under English domination, with groups in power ruthlessly shifting alliances, while the dauphin, the future King Charles VII, passed his days and nights in games and merry-making with his courtiers.

Joan was only thirteen when she first heard a mysterious voice enveloped in blinding radiance; as time went on, there were more voices, which she was able to identify as Michael the Archangel (p. 70), Catherine of Siena (p. 64), Margaret (p. 41), and others. Little by little, it became clear that these voices were telling Joan to save France. Joan was illiterate, little more than a girl, and of the peasant class—what the saints were demanding of her was impossible, unthinkable. Joan could turn to no one, certainly not to her unapproachable father, but soon the voices became specific and irresistible: she must save France, "It is God who commands it."

In a first, failed attempt at contacting the French army, Joan was sent away, but not before she prophesied a grave defeat. When this came true, she was taken more seriously. She dressed in men's clothing—as her voices had told her to—and went to the

OPPOSITE: The Victorian translator, poet, and artist Dante Gabriel Rossetti created a portrait of angelic androgyny to depict Joan of Arc as she listens to the voices that would direct her destiny and that of France. Against a field of the royal French fleurs-de-lys, the focus of the painting seems to be Joan's strong, articulate hands.

king. Again, her devotion was met with suspicion and ridicule until she was questioned closely and finally approved by an ecclesiastical panel. Leading the French army, Joan, clad in white armor, spurred the troops to victory after victory, receiving an arrow in the shoulder in one engagement. More than once, prompted by her voices, she foretold the future.

With Joan by his side, the weak Charles was crowned king of France at Rheims in 1429—the peasant girl from Domrémy had successfully completed her seemingly impossible task. However, from that moment, undermined by Charles and beset by bad luck, Joan met defeat after defeat until she was finally captured by the Burgundian forces. Abandoned by Charles and his supporters, Joan was sold to the English, her death warrant as good as signed.

The English charges were heresy, witchcraft, and dressing in the clothes of the opposite sex. The notes of the trial, which survive, reveal Joan as intelligent, candid, humorous, and deeply religious, even as she argued desperately for her life. But Joan was uneducated, all but helpless in theological matters, and this allowed her interrogators to twist her statements. Twice, she backed down, terrified by the torments that awaited her. The first time, she didn't listen to her voices; another time, the tribunal, intimidated by her spiritual power, offered to abandon the charges of heresy and witchcraft if Joan would agree to wear women's dress once more. The frightened girl agreed, and a gown was left in her cell. The following morning Joan had once again found the resolve to obey her voices.

In the end, the church gave her over to the civil authorities, who condemned her for heresy. In 1431, Joan of Arc, not yet twenty years old, was burned at the stake in the Rouen marketplace. She died invoking the name of Jesus aloud, her eyes on a cross held up to her gaze. At least one bystander was gripped with the chill terror of damnation: John Tressart, close to Henry VI,

the king of England who was crowned king of France that year, was heard to exclaim: "We are lost: We have burned a saint!"

King Charles VII, who had done nothing during Joan's captivity, on two occasions acted to have the Maid of Orléans's

The River Jordan, where John has been baptizing penitents, is prominent in the solemn moment when Jesus reveals his identity to John.

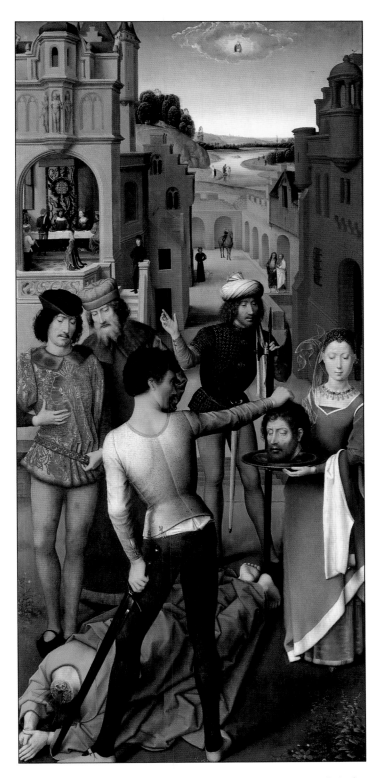

For all its aristocratic elegance, Hans Memling's depiction of Salome receiving the head of Saint John is full of emotion—Herod's frightened, pious horror and Salome's chilly but satisfied distaste.

reputation rehabilitated, but it was not until 1456, in response to a petition by Joan's mother and two brothers, that a papal commission found her verdict to have been reached by "fraud and deceit."

Joan of Arc is the patron saint of servicemen and servicewomen, and was traditionally invoked as the support of the common soldier; perhaps that is why, as a soldier betrayed by her king, she was canonized in 1920, following the mass deaths that flowed from the horror of World War I.

JOHN THE BAPTIST
JUNE 24

Zachariah, a priest of the Temple in Jerusalem, and his wife, Elizabeth, were holy people who had grown elderly in the service of the Lord. One day, Zachariah was alone in the sanctuary offering incense, when the angel Gabriel appeared to him and prophesied that Zachariah and Elizabeth, who had hitherto been barren, would have a son. Gabriel said that their son was to be named John and be especially dedicated to God from his birth; as an outward sign of this dedication, John would drink neither wine nor beer. Despite the wonder of the apparition and the angel's prophecy, Zachariah asked for a sign—and was struck dumb in reply, the angel telling him that he would remain so until John was born.

Elizabeth was a cousin of the Virgin Mary, who was already pregnant when she came to visit her kinswoman, herself six months along at the time. As the two women came together to embrace, Elizabeth felt the first stirrings within her. Mary stayed with Elizabeth for the last three months of her confinement, then helped deliver her cousin's child, the forerunner of her own. At the circumcision, those present urged the parents to name the child Zachariah, like his father, but when his father wrote down "John is his name," instantly he was able to speak again.

As a young man, John went into the desert to fast and prepare for his mission; in the empty wastes he prayed, dressed in animal skins, and ate only "wild honey and locusts." When he came out of the desert, he began to baptize those who confessed their sins in purification for the coming of the Messiah. And when Jesus himself appeared to be baptized by John, John

ABOVE: The late Renaissance painter Caravaggio (Michelangelo Merisi) was frequently criticized for his naturalistic portrayal of religious themes. Here, the down-to-earth and pious Martha, on the left, reproves her sister, the sensualist Mary Magdalene, for her frivolous attachment to worldly things.

fulfilled his angelic mission by pointing to Jesus and announcing, "This is the Lamb of God, who takes away the sin of the world."

Herod Antipas, one of the governors of Galilee, had married Herodias, his half brother's wife, who was also his niece; Herod's half brother was still living, and John rebuked the ruler publicly for his sin. Herod knew that John was holy, and the ruler was in awe of him and feared his followers. But Herod also shared his wife's great ambition, and he moved to silence the Baptist by having him beheaded on the occasion of a great feast in the year 29. Some say that Herod's stepdaughter Salome demanded the murder at her mother's instigation, others that Herod and Herodias conspired in the atrocity. The saint's beheading is commemorated on August 29.

Augustine (p. 112) noted that in most cases it is the day of a saint's death that is celebrated, the day in which they are born to eternal life. John the Baptist's celebration, an exception, marks his natal day, perhaps, again, as a foreshadowing of the Nativity of Christ. For Gabriel had foretold, "He shall be great before the Lord."

MARTHA

JULY 29

Martha; her sister, Mary Magdalene; and her brother, Lazarus, were close to Jesus, who raised Lazarus from the dead. Martha welcomed Christ as a guest in her home and lovingly looked after him. She is the patron saint of housekeepers and lay sisters.

There is a tradition that Martha, her brother and sister, and a number of other Christians were set adrift from what is now Israel in a rudderless boat with neither sails nor food. Landing safely in Marseilles, France, they traveled inland to Aix, where Martha's preaching converted many. In a woods on the banks of the Rhône River lived a dragon, "half animal and half fish," that had also come by sea, but from Asia. The inhabitants of the region came to Martha, pleading with her to rid them of the foul creature that killed people and sank ships.

Martha sprinkled the unholy beast with holy water and made the sign of the cross over him; as he was thus overcome, the people easily killed the dragon with spears and stones. Martha elected

to remain in that place, and there she prayed and fasted; in time a community of women gathered around her. Her death was revealed to her a year ahead, and during that last year she received angelic visitations. When her hour came, she asked to be carried outside so that she might see the beauty of the heavens one last time. She also asked that the Passion according to Saint Luke be read to her, and at the words "Father, into Thy hands I commend my spirit" she breathed her last.

RITA OF CASCIA

MAY 22

Although it was her heartfelt desire to become a nun, Rita, a young peasant girl born in Roccaporena, Italy, in 1377, married according to her parents' wishes. The marriage was a difficult one—both her husband and her sons were depraved and violent—but Rita was able to endure through her prayers. In time, her husband gave up his cruel and sinful ways, but she was unable to enjoy his transformation for, shortly after, he was murdered. Rita's sons sought vengeance, but in desperation she prayed that they might die rather than kill, and her prayers were answered: they fell ill and did not live to fulfill their purpose. Rita's prayers and faith brought the dying young men peace, and they passed on in Christian forgiveness.

Widowed and childless, Rita entered a convent of Augustinian nuns at Cascia, but only after persevering and overcoming the obstacles presented by her status—the convent only accepted virgins. Three times she petitioned to be received, and three times she was refused, until at last her sincere desire to give her life to God prevailed. Rita had always found solace for her sufferings in those of the Lord. Now a bride of Christ, the radiant love that had sustained her in the world shone even more brightly in her new life, which she marked with mortifications of the flesh made in the name of the Passion of Christ.

One day, as she meditated upon the Crown of Thorns, a wound appeared on her forehead exactly like the raw mark of a thorn upon her flesh; she bore the mark until her death in Cascia, Italy, in 1447. It is said that a rose blossomed out of season in order to comfort her in her last hours, and for this reason the rose is her symbol. Like Jude (p.23), Rita is patron saint of desperate situations.

✝ H E R E S A O F L I S I E U X

OCTOBER I

Born in Alençon, France, in 1873, Marie-Françoise-Thérèse was the youngest of the five surviving daughters of Louis Martin and Azélie-Marie Guérin. In Theresa's fourth year, her mother died, and the family moved to Lisieux, where her eldest sister entered the Carmelite convent when Theresa was nine. Already, the small, golden-haired child was attracted to the religious life; even at nine, she was no longer the boisterous, greedy child of her younger years.

Nearly five years later, when another sister entered the convent, Theresa's vocation became irresistible. (In time, four of the five sisters would enter the Carmelite Order in Lisieux.) A novice at fifteen, her resolution and piety argued in favor of her acceptance at such a young age, and she impressed her sisters in Christ by her bearing. Photographs show her as small and not strong, but she was dispensed only from the requirement to fast; she performed the other physical mortifications without complaint, picturing Christ beseeching her to sacrifice. She would later state: "I have reached the point of not being able to suffer any more—because all suffering is sweet to me." She died of tuberculosis on September 30, 1897, at twenty-four years old.

Theresa-of-the-Child-Jesus set out to be a saint, in all humility, a paradox she resolved in a life of prayerful and active holiness. "I am a very little soul," she wrote in her *Story of a Soul*, set down at her prioress' request, "who can only offer very little things to our Lord." Pope Pius XI beatified Theresa in 1923, and canonized her in 1925, in consideration of the spontaneous groundswell cult that arose upon her death and of the miracles that were attributable to her intercession.

Z I ✝ A

APRIL 27

Zita was born in 1218 in Monte Sagrati, Italy, into a religious, working-class home. When she was of age, she went out to work as a maid in the home of a prosperous weaver, Pagano di Fatinelli, and his family in Lucca, the nearest city. There, Zita folded her devotions into her daily life,

attending the earliest Mass daily, as well as performing her duties conscientiously, believing that work itself was a religious devotion. She was particularly sensitive to the corporal acts of mercy, giving much of her food to the hungry and sleeping on the floor because she had given her mattress away. She found serenity in her charity and in her round of tasks, but her fellow servants resented Zita's piety.

The miracles that attended her life were of a piece with her unassuming, concrete spiritual practice. One day, she heard that her master, a hot-tempered man, was about to inventory the family's supply of beans. In terror, Zita—who had formed the perhaps overzealous habit of giving away not only her own food but also her employer's stores—could only pray. When Pagano finished his review, he declared that all was as it should be. On another occasion, it happened that Zita lost track of time in church on a baking day; when she returned, in a panic, she found the loaves she had neglected to prepare miraculously ready for baking.

One bitterly cold Christmas, Zita was determined to attend Mass despite the weather. Pagano lent her his fur cloak, which she in turn promptly lent to a man shivering in the doorway of the church, telling him that she would reclaim it on her way out. After Mass, there was no one in the doorway, and Zita was obliged to return home without her master's valuable cloak. Pagano was enraged, until, some hours later, a man appeared at the door, returned the cloak to Zita in the presence of members of the household, then disappeared. All those present felt touched by a heavenly exaltation, and ever since then, the doorway in the Church of San Frediano, where Zita performed her act of trust and mercy, has been known as *la porta dell'angelo*—the Door of the Angel.

Zita's patience, industriousness, and modest good sense earned her the family's esteem, an attention as painful to her simplicity as the earlier unkindness of the other servants. Her new position in the family, as companion and adviser, allowed her to devote more time to her works of mercy, so that she cared not only for the ill and poor but for the jailed as well, especially those condemned to death, for whom she fervently prayed. After forty-eight years in the service of God, through her service to the weaver's family, Zita died an easeful death at sixty years old, in 1278. Her emblem is a set of keys, and she is the patron saint of domestic servants.

This photograph of Theresa of Lisieux after her first communion shows the open-hearted sweetness for which the saint was celebrated.

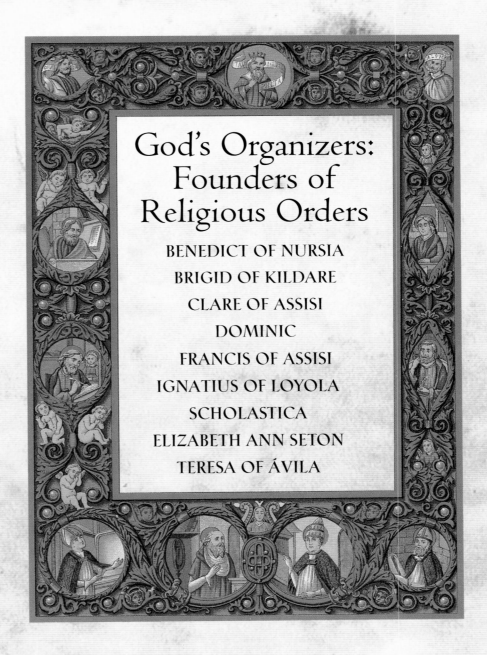

CHAPTER EIGHT

God's Organizers: Founders of Religious Orders

BENEDICT OF NURSIA

BRIGID OF KILDARE

CLARE OF ASSISI

DOMINIC

FRANCIS OF ASSISI

IGNATIUS OF LOYOLA

SCHOLASTICA

ELIZABETH ANN SETON

TERESA OF ÁVILA

THROUGHOUT THE HISTORY OF THE CATHOLIC CHURCH, THE FOUNDERS OF ORDERS OF RELIGIOUS COMMUNITIES HAVE PLAYED A SPECIAL PART IN HELPING THE FAITHFUL KEEP THEIR HEARTS AND MINDS ON GOD. NOT ONLY DID THESE SAINTS DEVOTE THEIR LIVES TO GOD, BUT THEY ENABLED OTHERS TO LIVE FOR GOD'S GLORY WITHIN THEIR ORDERS.

BENEDICT OF NURSIA

JULY 11

Benedict's parents sent him from his native Nursia, today Norcia, Italy, where he was born at the end of the fifth century, to Rome to continue his education, but he fled the corruptions of the city for solitude in a cave in Subiaco, several days' journey away. News of his piety reached a nearby community of monks, who asked him to be their abbot. Despite his reservations, Benedict agreed, but before long some of the brothers, unwilling to accept a stricter regime than they were used to, tried to poison him. When Benedict made the sign of the Cross over the poisoned cup of wine they gave him, it shattered.

In time, Benedict founded twelve monasteries; he also, according to tradition, built a church dedicated to John the Baptist (p. 91) from a temple of Apollo and converted many in the area. Some of the tales told of Benedict's struggles with the Devil concern the raising of this church. Once, the brothers went to lift a particular stone but could not. Benedict made the sign of the Cross over it, and the brothers were able to lift it easily—proving that the Devil had been sitting on it. Another time, the Evil One caused a wall to fall and kill a novice, but Benedict prayed over the youth's broken body and restored him to life.

Benedict's faith was steadfast and serene. It happened that there was a desperate famine in Campania, the region of one of Benedict's monasteries. The friars, seeing that they had only five loaves of bread left, became frightened. Benedict chided them gently, saying, "Why do you trouble yourselves over so insignificant a matter? Today bread is wanting, but there is no reason to fear that tomorrow you will not have it in plenty." And, indeed, the following morning, a great quantity of flour appeared at the threshold of the founder's cell—its source was never ascertained.

In 547, when the great founder knew he was dying, he had himself carried into the chapel, where he received Holy Communion standing, supported by his brothers, before giving his soul to God. He and his sister, Scholastica (p. 106), who some say was his twin, were interred in a common grave.

Some of the tales of Benedict's life portray him as impatient with those more imperfect than he; strong-willed and filled as he was with an unshakable trust in God, he required obedience and simple faith from his monks. His rule, however, has come down to us, and it is filled with a love of humanity that embraces

PAGES 96 AND 97: The subject of Lorenzo Lotto's 1606 painting The Sermon of Saint Dominic *seems to be Dominic's eloquence, reflected in his audience's fixed attention. The founder of the Order of Preachers wears the order's white habit and black cloak; the flames more likely refer to Dominic's most famous miracle than to the more sinister bonfires of the Inquisition.*

OPPOSITE: Hans Memling's Benedict is an unlikely revolutionary, but his monastic rule was far more humane than the harsh requirements of earlier orders.

SANCTVS
BENEDICTVS

the infinite variety of God's creation. Benedict described his rule as a "school of the Lord's service, in which we hope to order nothing harsh or rigorous."

BRIGID OF KILDARE

FEBRUARY I

Brigid was born in northeastern Ireland around 450, the daughter of a mother named Brocca and a father named Dubthac. Converted by Patrick (p. 81), she probably became a nun when she was still very young, and a number of miracles of nurturing and healing are attributed to her, including restoring sight to several people. Having made a vow of chastity, she prayed to God to disfigure her in the face of her parents' insistence that she marry. God obliged, and she suffered a "melted" eye.

She founded an important nunnery at Kildare; it was very likely a double monastery, that is, a community of friars as well as nuns, over which Brigid presided. She was tremendously respected—one early source even refers to her as a bishop. Whatever the historical facts, Brigid was—and is—beloved: her legend is one of the richest of all the saints', forming a portrait of a generous, radiant soul.

Her holiness was recognized during her lifetime, and her group of followers, reaching into England, Scotland, and beyond, blossomed after her death around 523, with beautiful tales of her great compassion. One story relates that, when still a girl at home, Brigid was sent to collect butter; on the way back, she gave it all away to the poor. When she returned home, concerned about how to explain what she had done, she discovered that everything she had given away was replaced and more.

Brigid and Patrick were "the columns on which all Ireland rested." Sometime during the Danish incursions of the eighth through eleventh centuries, Brigid's relics were moved from Kildare to Downpatrick, where they are believed to be interred side by side with Patrick's remains.

This anonymous painting of Clare and eight episodes of her life was made not long after the saint's canonization, which took place within two years of her death. The artist was seeking to portray her spiritual, not individual, likeness.

CLARE OF ASSISI

AUGUST 11

Chiara Offreduccio, the daughter of Ortolana di Fiumi and Faverone Offreduccio, was raised in the noble style to which she had been born in 1194. As a girl in Assisi, Italy, she twice refused proposals of marriage, but it was not until she heard Francis (p. 102) preach at the Lenten services that she knew what course she wanted her life to take. She found a way to talk secretly, away from her disapproving parents, with Francis, who recognized the depth of her vocation. On Palm Sunday, Clare ran away from home, repairing to the house where Francis lived with his brother friars, and there she made private vows. Francis cut off her hair, and before the altar, Clare traded her sumptuous gown for a sackcloth robe girdled with coarse rope.

At first, Clare was received at a Benedictine nunnery through Francis's offices. There, with the sisters' support, she withstood the efforts of her family and friends to bring her home to Assisi. Next, Francis helped Clare enter a second convent, where her sister Agnes, though only fifteen years old, also took the habit from Francis, as Clare had done. (Agnes was also canonized later.)

Finally, again with Francis's help, Clare, Agnes, and a small number of other women formed a house by the Church of San Damiano, just outside Assisi. Francis appointed Clare to be the superior of the convent, for which he wrote a "rule of life," outlining how the sisters were to conduct themselves. They became the Poor Ladies, or, in England, the Minoresses, from the name of Francis's community, the Friars Minor; today, the order is known as the Poor Clares. Some three years later, Pope Innocent III granted Clare the "privilege of poverty," that is, he allowed the nuns to live entirely on charity, owning nothing either individually or in common. In time, other ecclesiastical authorities would criticize the sisters' vow as imprudent, but Clare fought for her vision.

Clare combined remarkable, seemingly contradictory attributes: she was one of the Church's most revered contemplatives, yet she ran her house efficiently, founded several more, and directed the founders of still other convents of the order. She was reluctant to assume the leadership of her house and her order, yet on one occasion when the nunnery of the Poor Ladies and the town of Assisi were under military attack, Clare—whose particular devotion was to the Eucharist—repelled the hostile forces by holding up a monstrance, displaying the consecrated Host. (This became one of her emblems in art, though she is also represented holding a lily or a cross, or, as founder of her order, a crozier.) The sisters ate no meat, wore nothing on their feet, and slept on the ground, yet Clare sometimes tucked her nuns in as they slept, and she advised the founder of a house in Prague to beware of overzealousness in asceticism, "for our bodies are not made of brass." Committed to obedience, she nonetheless stood up to the Holy See itself to defend the Poor Clares' "privilege of poverty," and Pope Innocent IV came to attend her twice during her last illness. Her feast day commemorates not the date of her death in 1253, but that of her burial.

DOMINIC

AUGUST 7

The birth of Domingo de Guzmán in Calaruega, Spain, in 1170 was preceded by portents: when his mother, Joanna, was pregnant with him, she dreamed of a little dog bearing a lit torch. This later became one of the saint's emblems, along with the star that his godmother saw on his brow immediately after he was baptized.

Dominic studied and prayed, and by virtue of his scholarship and piety was named a canon regular of the cathedral of Osma when he was twenty-six. Armed with knowledge and a profound compassion for those lost to heresy, he joined an informal mission to convert the Albigensians of southern France, a heretic group so deeply rooted and belligerent that there was virtual civil war in that region. While a number of orthodox prelates advocated a military response to the rebellious sect, Dominic responded with a more spiritual tack, saying: "The enemies of the faith cannot be overcome like that. Arm yourself with prayer rather than a sword." He added, perhaps as a subtle reminder of some of the Albigensian criticisms of the established Church, "Wear humility rather than fine clothes."

Several of the countless miracles attributed to Dominic reflect the power of his learning. It is said, for example, that he once wrote down a series of arguments refuting Albigensianism and sent the paper to members of the sect, who decided to put the power of the Church to the test. Three times they threw the

paper into the fire, and three times the paper leaped out intact. Another time, Dominic dropped some of his books into a stream; three days later they reappeared—perfectly dry—at the end of a fisherman's hook. Yet, when the intellectually powerful Dominic was asked what book he studied most, he replied, "The book of love."

Learning and simple piety proved an effective combination. Dominic founded the Friars Preachers, an order that followed the Augustinian rule: the friars lived lives of chastity, poverty, and humility. A particularly endearing characteristic of Dominic's legend is his instant recourse to prayer in any quandary. Some of these problems might seem unspiritual, such as the time Dominic arrived late at a locked monastery. Reluctant to disturb his brothers but not knowing what else to do, he prayed— and found himself inside the monastery walls. Dominic had many visions, outwitted the Devil many times, and through exorcism freed many souls from the tyranny of demons.

The preacher was known for his even temper and kindness, and for being stricter with himself than with his brothers. Tales are told of his defeating his carnal desires and helping his brothers to continence and chastity, yet he was a friend to women. Only his heartfelt compassion ruffled his well-known even temper: he resisted the excesses of the early Inquisition, refusing, for example, to condone secular–religious alliances in the courts. Myriad stories of healing, both spriritual and physical, are attributed to him, both before and after his death (in Bologna, Italy, in 1221), and a recurring image in his legend is that

of a sweet odor that wafted from his person. His cult was vastly popular throughout Italy; the date of the translation of his relics was at one time observed as an important feast day as far south as Sicily.

FRANCIS OF ASSISI
OCTOBER 4

Born Giovanni Bernardone in Assisi, Italy, in 1181, he was called Francesco, "the Frenchman," because his father, a prosperous cloth merchant, had been in France on business at the time of his birth. Like many young people of means—his mother, Pica, may have been a Provençale lady of gentle birth—Francis was pleasure-loving and reckless, and came to his vocation in stages. Francis was taken as a prisoner of war to nearby Perugia, during the war between that city and his native Assisi. Held for a year, he first received his calling in an enemy cell. Upon returning home, he fell gravely ill, displaying during his long convalescence an uncharacteristic patience that rendered his character sturdier than before. Experiencing a series of dreams and visions, Francis became increasingly distracted. He was teased about being in love, to which he replied, "Yes, I am going to take a wife more beautiful and worthy than any you know." (Throughout his life, Francis would retain a joyful lightheartedness

Francis is shown holding a copy of the Gospel: his order was established at first as a small group of wandering preachers who owned nothing, even in common.

Giotto's fresco in Francis's church in Assisi shows the saint receiving the stigmata on Monte La Verna. The dramatic landscape of this work seems to express the shock and importance of the event.

and a simple, steadfast faith despite physical pain and fierce, Devil-driven temptations.)

At prayer one day in the Church of Saint Damian, the young man thrice heard a voice saying from the direction of the crucifix: "Francis, repair my falling house." The ever-practical Francis took goods from his family's stores, sold them, and gave the money to the priest of Saint Damian's. His father angrily fetched him home, shackled him, and kept Francis a prisoner until Pica released her son in her husband's absence—whereupon Francis serenely went to "wed Lady Poverty." (He later returned the money to his father, but only after a high prelate obliged him to.) Francis was so devoted to his bride that he sometimes suffered pangs of envy toward those poorer than he, though he himself wore rags.

When Francis was almost thirty, Pope Innocent III granted him the authority to found a community, the Friars Minor, whose members owned nothing, even in common, but lived only by the charity of others. The brothers traveled throughout Italy preaching simplicity, penitence, and a glad and loving faith. The friaries multiplied, and two years later, in 1212, Francis and Clare founded the order of the Poor Ladies, later to be known as the Poor Clares, a series of religious communities for women espousing the Franciscan way of life.

Francis dreamed of converting the Muslims, and in 1219, he voyaged to Egypt with a group of crusaders. He visited the Holy Land, but returned to Italy with his hope unfulfilled, though others of his order went to Morocco and elsewhere as missionaries, often finding martyrdom.

Francis's vision of God embraced every living thing in its vastness and unity—there are many tales of his gently asking "sister birds" to cease their singing while he prayed, and of his tender care for the lives of earthworms. His resplendent *Canticle of the Sun* expresses his all-encompassing love for God's creation, from Brother Sun to Sister Moon.

In 1224, as he prayed, Francis received the stigmata—five wounds identical to those suffered by Christ on the cross. In his modesty, he hid them, but they caused him intense pain for the two remaining years of his life. When, in 1226, after a long illness, he felt the end to be near, he welcomed Sister Death.

Francis performed many miracles of healing and transformation during his lifetime, and many more miracles occurred through his intercession after his death.

ĊGNAṪIVS OF LOYOLA

JULY 31

Íñigo de Oñaz y Loyola was born around 1491, in Loyola, Guipúzcoa, Spain, the youngest of the eleven children of an ancient and noble family of the Basque provinces in the north of Spain. He went to war as a knight and was seriously wounded in both legs in the defense of Pamplona; he limped for the rest of his life. Growing restless as he convalesced, he asked for romances, the highly colored historical novels of heroes, love,

and adventure so popular at the time. Instead, he was given a book on the life of Jesus, and another on legends of the saints.

Gradually, he became intrigued, then inspired by the books, giving himself over to penitences, including physical mortifications. Over the next year, following a pilgrimage to Monserrat, near Barcelona, Ignatius lived in retirement, sometimes in a house of Dominican friars, sometimes among the poor, sometimes alone in a cave. During this time, he began composing his timeless *Spiritual Exercises.*

Next, he made his way to Jerusalem. Though he intended to stay and be a missionary, his family's wealth and position made him an attractive target for kidnapping. Out of consideration for his family, Ignatius returned to Europe and began a ten-year course of study, which took him from Barcelona to Paris. His gentle corrections and warm manner brought back to the Church many who had strayed, but twice he was imprisoned by the ecclesiastical authorities under suspicion of unorthodoxy. In Paris, Ignatius gathered around him six friends (including Francis Xavier [p. 78]); together they practiced his spiritual exercises and determined to go preach in Palestine if they could. If they could not, they vowed they would serve God as directed by the pope.

The ardent group arrived in Venice but found no ships to take them to the Holy Land. They turned to Pope Paul III, and those who had not yet been ordained now were. In Rome, Ignatius and his friends petitioned the pope to approve their holy order—in Paris, they had already taken vows of poverty and chastity; they now proposed two more vows, one of obedience to a general superior, himself answerable directly to the pope, and the other to go as missionaries as directed by the Holy Father. The order was approved in 1540; the following year, Ignatius was named the first general superior of the Society of Jesus, or Jesuits.

Ignatius spent the rest of his life—the next sixteen years—in Rome; his *Spiritual Exercises* were published in 1548. By the time he died, in 1556, the order he and nine friends (three more had joined the original six) had founded numbered one thousand members, who worked as educators and missionaries throughout Europe and in India and Brazil. Yet the Church remembers Ignatius best for his private spirituality: he is the patron saint of spritual exercises and retreats.

OPPOSITE: Saint Ignatius casts out devils in Peter Paul Rubens's vivid painting of 1617–18. His hand on the altar shows where his power comes from.

ABOVE: An artist from the region of their birth painted this tender conversation between Scholastica and Benedict. According to tradition, Scholastica was far from being the meek lady portrayed here.

SCHOLASTICA

FEBRUARY 10

Little is known about this spritually strong-willed saint, who was born in Norcia, Italy, around the year 480. She was Benedict's sister—tradition has it she was his twin—and herself founded a convent near Monte Cassino, Italy, of which she was the abbess. She and her brother had always been very close; now they both lived lives wholly dedicated to God. Once a year they met near her convent to talk of their great happiness. On one occasion, Scholastica could not bear for their conversation to be interrupted and she pleaded with Benedict to stay so that they might go on talking all night. He refused, but Scholastica prayed—and a tremendous, howling tempest arose, forcing Benedict to remain. It was to be the last of their spiritual dialogues, for Scholastica, the "mother" of nuns of the Benedictine order, died three days later near Monte Cassino, in the year 543. When Benedict himself passed on, some four years after his sister, he was buried with her; as Saint Gregory wrote: "so death did not separate the bodies of these two, whose minds had ever been united in the Lord."

ELIZABETH
ANN SETON

JANUARY 4

Elizabeth Ann Bayley was born in 1774, the daughter of a socially prominent professor at King's College, today Columbia University, in New York. She was the stepsister of the Episcopalian Archbishop James Roosevelt Bayley of Baltimore, and was herself a practicing Episcopalian, like everyone she knew of her class, though Elizabeth was particularly devout. In 1794, she married a merchant, William Seton, and in 1797, with other philanthropic ladies, Elizabeth founded the Society for the Relief of Poor Widows with Small Children. Elizabeth and her husband were happy together and had five children, but in the early 1800s, ill fortune struck—William Seton lost all his money, and his health began to fail.

The family traveled to Leghorn, Italy, where they had friends, in hopes that the climate might restore William's health, but he died there in 1803. Elizabeth's friends sustained her, and

Elizabeth "Mother" Seton was the first native-born American to be canonized. This portrait captures the mix of contemplation and determination that she brought to the founding of her order.

it was during that period that she became attracted to the Catholic faith, considered low-class in her American circle. Two years later, Elizabeth Ann Seton was baptized in New York, whereupon her family and friends refused to acknowledge her. Nearly penniless and abandoned by the only world and support she knew, Elizabeth was asked to open a girls' school in Baltimore under the auspices of the Church. The organization she gave the school she founded in 1809 would form the basis for parochial schools in the United States from then on. Her intelligence, education, breeding, and natural charm were great assets, accompanied as they were by a great clarity and firmness of purpose; yet Elizabeth also suffered deeply during periods in which she felt distant from God.

Also in 1809, Elizabeth and four associates founded a small religious community in Emmitsburg, in northern Maryland; the women cared for the sick and poor and taught children. "Mother" Seton was the first superior of the order, from when it received its rule in 1812 until her death. She and eighteen others took their vows in 1813, thus officially establishing the American Sisters of Charity of Saint Vincent de Paul. Her position of authority, so repugnant to her sensibility, provided Mother Seton with a constant spiritual challenge, which she embraced. She would live to see the establishment of some twenty houses of her order before she died in Emmitsburg in 1821, at the age of forty-six.

TERESA OF ÁVILA

OCTOBER 15

Teresa de Cepeda y Ahumada was born in Ávila, Spain, in 1515, into a large, happy, healthy, wealthy, and pious family. She herself was imaginative, outgoing, and fervent. Even as a child, she displayed zeal for the religious life: she and her brother Rodrigo ran away from home once, intending to go to the land of the Moors and find martyrdom. (They were found down the road by an uncle and returned home.)

Her mother died when Teresa was fourteen, and in her grief she lost her spiritual direction, reading romances and adorning herself with fripperies. Concerned, Teresa's father sent her to a convent in the city, but she fell ill and returned home. During her long recovery, she read the *Letters* of the learned Saint Jerome (p. 113), and these inspired her to enter a convent—this time for life.

The sisters of the Carmelite Convent of the Incarnation were high-born and social, and Teresa, who had given herself to the practice of mental prayer, was distracted by the gregarious life: the nuns received guests, owned personal possessions, and paid visits outside the convent walls when they chose. Furthermore, Teresa was charming, intelligent, and warm-hearted, so it was difficult for her to find the solitude her soul craved.

Once again, she fell ill, this time for more than three years, and resumed her practice of mental prayers and other disciplines. She humbly sought the aid of spiritual directors and, in time, experienced an overwhelming interior transformation. She came to identify with Mary Magdalene (p. 121) and Augustine (p. 112), who became examples of penance. Her visions and ecstasies grew stronger; on one occasion, she felt an angel piercing her heart with divine love. After twenty-five years in the large, worldly Convent of the Incarnation, she hungered for simplicity.

Teresa was deeply mystical, but also down-to-earth and witty—a driver reported that as she pulled herself together after their carriage overturned, she exclaimed to God, "No wonder you have so few friends, since this is the way you treat them!" She founded seventeen houses of a reformed, or "barefoot," Carmelite order, two of them monasteries. She had a brush with the Inquisition, overcame secular political obstacles, won over adversaries within her order, and conquered her own ill health in her determination to create small, hardworking communities dedicated to prayer and solitude. In 1582, returning from Burgos, where she had just established her seventeenth house, Teresa was taken ill and passed away.

She wrote, at her confessors' behest, her life; *The Way of Perfection*, for her spiritual daughters; the *Book of Foundations*, describing the establishment of her beloved houses; and *The Interior Castle*, the remarkable account of her inner journey to God; along with other writings. In 1970, she was named a Doctor of the Church, along with Catherine of Siena (p. 64). Popularly, she is invoked in cases of headache and heart attacks.

Not strictly speaking barefoot, but enough to recall her reformation of the Carmelite order, Teresa appears lit by the internal radiance of spiritual rapture.

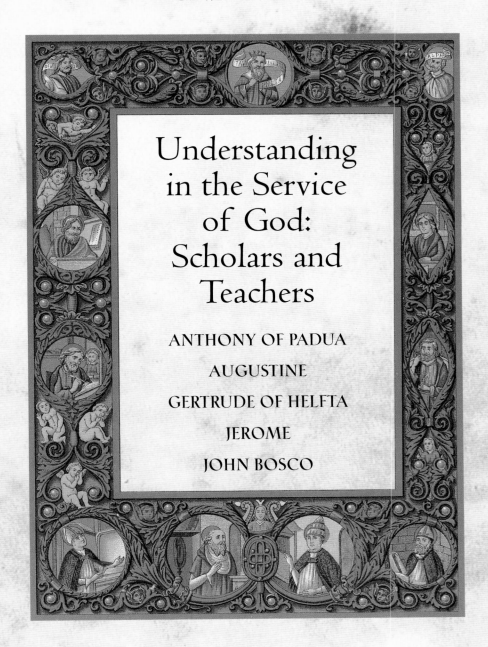

Chapter Nine

Understanding in the Service of God: Scholars and Teachers

ANTHONY OF PADUA

AUGUSTINE

GERTRUDE OF HELFTA

JEROME

JOHN BOSCO

THE CHURCH HAS ALWAYS HONORED THE APOSTLES AND OTHER MISSIONARIES WHO HAVE TAKEN THE TRUE RELIGION TO THE PAGANS. BEGINNING IN THE FOURTH CENTURY, SCHOLARS ALSO BECAME CRUCIAL TO THE SALVATION OF THOSE WHO WOULD OTHERWISE BE LED INTO THEOLOGICAL ERROR THAT WOULD DAMN THEM IN THE NEXT WORLD. THE SCHOLARS AND TEACHERS DISCUSSED IN THIS CHAPTER BROUGHT PEOPLE CLOSER TO GOD IN A VARIETY OF WAYS; THROUGH PERSONAL TOUCH, BY MAKING INTELLECTUAL WRITINGS MORE ACCESSIBLE, AND BY REACHING OUT TO THEIR FELLOW CHRISTIANS.

ANTHONY OF PADUA

JUNE 13

Born in Lisbon, Portugal, around 1193, the son of wealthy parents, Anthony entered an Augustinian monastery as a canon regular, but when he was twenty-five, he was seized with a desire to go to Morocco and serve God as a missionary among the Muslims and perhaps find martyrdom. To this end, he was received by the Franciscan order, but of his three aims, he fulfilled only the first—he then fell ill, and eventually sailed for home.

A storm turned the ship eastward, and Anthony landed at Messina, in Sicily. He traveled north to Assisi to attend the general chapter, or meeting, of the Franciscans that was to take place there, and it was soon discovered that Anthony had a marvelous eloquence that made this shortish, sickly, and some-what pudgy man a popular speaker. His passionate yet simple sincerity and his remarkable learning and captivating eloquence were irresistible, and he converted large numbers of heretics. His greatest joys were in the number of sinners who returned to the church and in the ever-growing loving kindness evident in the daily life of Padua, his adopted city.

His health, which had never been strong, finally failed him on his way home from preaching a series of sermons in 1231. The people of Padua, whom he had so loved, thronged his funeral with fervent demonstrations of affection and grief.

He is known as "the Wonderworker," for the many miracles reported after his death, and is frequently portrayed holding the Christ Child. He is often looked to as the celebrated finder of lost articles, perhaps because of a tale in which the saint appeared to a monk who had stolen a goblet. (The terrified friar forthwith returned the precious vessel.)

PAGES 108 AND 109: People associate Anthony of Padua with small children, because of his vision of holding the Christ Child. In this episode from an altarpiece, Piero della Francesca captures the humble solemnity of one of Anthony's miracles.

OPPOSITE: In Francisco de Zurbarán's Saint Anthony of Padua with the Christ Child *of 1640, the artist idealizes the saint's homely appearance, but conveys Anthony's legendary tenderness.*

AUGUSTINE
AUGUST 28

From childhood, Augustine was vivacious and impulsive, with a spiritual hunger as compelling as his sensual appetites. He was born in Tagste, Numidia, in 354, in what is today Souk-Ahras, Algeria, to a fervently Christian mother, Monica (p. 81), and a pagan Roman father, Patricius. Augustine, one of three children, was raised in his mother's faith, though he was not baptized, for his mother—concerned above all for her son's soul—believed that his sins would weigh all the more grievously if committed after baptism. He was a lively, mischievous child, who cheated at games, stole fruit, and was enthralled by the sights and scents of the world around him, as he would later confess.

Even as a young man, Augustine was both honest and stubborn, respecting his spiritual instincts as obdurately as he did his intellectual dissatisfactions. He was just as sincere in his prayers: in his *Confessions*, he revealed that as a teenager torn between spiritual and earthly desire, he had prayed: "Give me chastity and continence—but not just yet."

At sixteen, the ambitious young man went on to Carthage, the intellectual center of North Africa, to study law, and almost immediately took a mistress. In Carthage, a jewel of the Roman Empire, he studied the great writers and speakers of the Classical ages (he disliked Greek and loved Latin), and it was Cicero that turned Augustine toward philosophy.

At this time, Augustine believed in God but rejected Christian teachings; he converted to Manichaeism, an ascetic religion that held that evil and good were the two equal First Principles. As time went on, the young seeker became increasingly impressed with the learned Christians who could counter the arguments of the Manichaeans, but, as he wrote, "I was unable to conceive of any but material realities."

In Rome, where Augustine went to teach literature and public speaking, spiritual hungers consumed him, driving him toward despair, for his beliefs no longer sustained him, and there seemed to be nothing to take their place. In Milan, he was drawn to the future Saint Ambrose, the city's bishop, first by his kindness and warmth and only secondly by the charms of his sermons—though Augustine steadfastly rejected their content.

But his dissatisfaction with his chosen religion had opened the door. In Milan, Augustine embraced Neoplatonism, a philosophy that brought him to accept a nonmaterial truth. Once he accepted a spiritual reality, his soul made the leap to Christianity; he and his son, Adeodatus, were baptized the same day. Because of his Manichaean past, Augustine was able to convert many of its believers to Christianity. His writings are among the most famous of all time and earned him the title of Doctor of the Church.

He returned home to Africa, where he founded a monastic order. Reluctantly but humbly, he obeyed the church's invitation to be ordained; five years later, he was made a bishop and served his community with fervor and faith for thirty-four years, until his death in Hippo, Numidia, in 430.

ABOVE: Augustine—by his own account—was far more human than he appears in Bartolommeo di Giovanni's painting, in which he holds the instruments of his enduring mission. Augustine's works are still widely read today.

GERTRUDE OF HELFTA
NOVEMBER 16

Born in 1256 of unknown parents and background, Gertrude was raised from the age of five by the nuns of the convent of Helfta, which was either Benedictine or Cistercian. Gertrude would be inspired all her life by Saint Francis of Assisi. In the convent, she was under the tutelage of Saint Mechtilde, the convent chorister—"a nightingale of Christ." Their spiritual experiences were collected together as *The Revelations of Gertrude and Mechtilde*, which includes *The Herald of God's Loving-Kindness*, written in part by Gertrude herself.

Gertrude received a humanistic education notable for its breadth and depth. The best of the era, it includes the ancient authors, and she excelled in scholarship. She took the veil, becoming a nun in the cloister where she had grown up, and which she very likely never left. In her mid-twenties, she experienced the first of the mystical visions that influenced her writings and turned her life from one of "lukewarm prayers" to one of contemplation and a ceaseless striving for perfect holiness. As she was preparing for bed one night, Gertrude saw Christ and heard him speak to her, promising, "I will save and deliver you. Fear not." In later years, she wrote, "I was led to correct my faults by the sweetness of His love far more than by fear of His just anger."

Like Jerome, Gertrude put away her beloved secular authors in favor of the Bible; Doctors of the Church such as Augustine, Saint Gregory, and Saint Bernard; and the Liturgy, that is, the texts of the Mass and other celebrations. With Saint Mechtilde, she had a particular devotion to the Sacred Heart and to Saint Joseph, and was among the first to practice frequent communion.

Gertrude had been very ill for some ten years when she died at forty-five years old, on November 17, 1302. Her writings reveal her theological and mystical insights, the visions she experienced, and her increasing charity and faith in God's love, as her soul opened toward eternity. For her theological writings and her mysticism, she is known today as Saint Gertrude the Great.

JEROME

SEPTEMBER 30

Jerome was born in 342, in Stridon, Dalmatia, a town not far from Aquileia, which was, at the time, one of the richest cities in northern Italy. Raised in a Christian family, the boy learned the rudiments of religion and letters before being sent to Rome to perfect his education. There, he studied Latin and Greek and fell under the spell of the rhetorical elegance of the great classical authors—a weakness he would never overcome.

Though young Jerome never succumbed to the sins so readily available in the capital of the empire, he was rather lazy about his religious practice—paradoxes were characteristic of this great Doctor of the Church. As was the custom at the time, he was baptized as an adult at eighteen after an extensive period of instruction, though he actually experienced his true spiritual awakening a few years later. Returning to the area of his birth in his late twenties, Jerome stayed in Aquileia, whose bishop was surrounded with the best of the clergy of western Europe.

The young scholar was already a person of strong feelings, and controversial, when after a few years, the group around the bishop disbanded. Jerome resolved to travel eastward to Antioch, and then, following a delirium-induced vision that affected him profoundly, to the desert near that city. There, his later letters reported, he was plagued by poor health and tormented by searing carnal desires, which he defeated with weeks of fasting and prayer. In addition, he took up the study of Hebrew and reluctantly became embroiled in church politics, which resulted in his equally reluctant ordination.

From Antioch, Jerome went to Constantinople to study the Holy Scriptures, and from the Byzantine capital he traveled back to Rome, where he revised the Latin translation of the New Testament at Pope Damasus' behest. (Because of his work for the Pope, he is often depicted wearing a cardinal's hat—as if he were a high-ranking prelate—as well as accompanied by a lion from whose paw the saint is said to have removed a thorn.) At the same time, Jerome was gathering about him a remarkable group of ascetic Roman matrons, several of whom, such as Saint Paula, Saint Melania the Elder, and Saint Marcella, were later canonized. Here, too, Jerome's dual nature is revealed, for his writings on celibacy in particular reveal a deep-seated mistrust of, even contempt for, women, though he respected individual women greatly.

Jerome's attacks on the habits of the clergy and others were arrogant, biting denunciations that soon aroused resentment and vicious gossip, especially concerning Paula, the wealthy, wellborn lady closest to Jerome. Jerome and his spiritual family left Rome for Bethlehem, where Paula financed several buildings for religious communities, as well as a hospice and a school where Jerome taught children Latin and Greek. For a time there was peace, the climate suited him, and Jerome wrote lovingly of the many Christians who flocked to the Holy Land "and set us the example of every virtue."

Jerome's great work in these years was to translate into Latin, or rework existing Latin translations of, almost all of the Old Testament, and perhaps no one could have brought to the purpose both his passionate love of language and his transcendent spiritual

understanding. But these were troubled years, when Church doctrine was taking shape and even the most even-tempered engaged in incendiary correspondence—Jerome quarreled fiercely with Augustine, among others.

Jerome suffered a personal loss when Paula died in 404; shortly after, waves of barbarian invasions into Italy sent Romans fleeing to the Holy Land. The stern, generous, and compassionate scholar put aside his beloved translation, saying, "For today we must translate the words of the Scriptures into deeds." He could not have known that his own communities would suffer violent, even fatal reprisals from a heretical faction he had refused to countenance. In 420, Jerome, weary and sick but serene in his faith, passed into the Light at last.

JOHN BOSCO
JANUARY 31

Giovanni Melchior Bosco, born in Piemonte, Italy, in 1815, the youngest son of a peasant family, received his first vision in a dream when he was nine. His father had died seven years before, when John was only two, and his mother struggled to provide for the family. Still a child himself, a dream showed him his vocation: to bring poor boys like himself to God, with love always, never with verbal or physical violence. And indeed, he would report later in life, he didn't recall ever "formally punishing a boy"—much to the scandal of educators.

Bosco's own education had been hard won, and he was determined to teach poor boys to read and write. In time, he would extend their education to technical skills in order to save young apprentices from the adult temptations they faced as children and impressionable young men in a grown-up world.

His technical schools, along with his good humor, seemingly infinite patience, and understanding, brought kindness, hope, and a Christian way of life to thousands of difficult, even almost impossible, boys and young men. Bosco was a skilled acrobat and good at magic tricks: one story tells of him challenging a traveling

OPPOSITE: Being trusted by animals is an attribute of a number of saints. The lion Jerome helped by removing a thorn from its paw is prominent in Perugino's Saint Jerome Repenting *of 1515, along with the imaginatively depicted desert of the Holy Land.*

juggler to a contest on a Sunday. When John won, he led his urchins to church.

John was ordained in 1841, materially aided by his village—his very clothes were donated by the mayor, the parish priest, and various villagers. Known by his priestly honorific "Don," as his protégés called him, throughout his life Bosco followed the directions he received in his visions with a combination of hard work, practicality, and an unswerving, simple faith that was often rewarded with miracles. The miracles that attended Don Bosco's mission were in keeping with it: many were healed through his intercession, and there were instances of multiplication of food.

In 1859, Don Bosco founded what is today the worldwide order of the Salesians, named for his favorite saint, Francis de Sales. In 1872, with Saint Mary Mazzarello, Don Bosco founded the Daughters of Mary Help of Christians. There is also a third order of the Salesians made up of laypersons dedicated to the saint's work. The money that was required for his work always appeared, as did help from people at every level of society, even though Don Bosco and his cohorts labored in a militantly anticlerical nineteenth-century Italy. In that momentous period of Italy's unification, the king himself was one of the humble priest's supporters.

With all his activities, Don Bosco was extremely busy, though he always made time for a trip to the countryside with a group of boys, Mass in a local church, then a picnic and games. He was in great demand as a preacher and wrote several books in addition to his ongoing fund-raising and organizing. So effective was he that the pope requested his assistance in finishing construction of a church in honor of the Sacred Heart. When Don Bosco could find no more moneys in Italy, he went to France, a country with a special devotion to the Sacred Heart. The pope's basilica was built, and Don Bosco said a Mass shortly after it was consecrated in May of 1887.

About that time, Don Bosco became exhausted; for two years, he had been advised to slow down, to no avail. His health continued to fail, and Don Bosco, wonder-worker and healer of souls as well as bodies, passed away in Turin, Italy, in 1888. Forty thousand mourners paid their last respects in the church where the saint's body lay, and the people of Turin, many of them the boys he had helped, lined the streets to honor him as his coffin was carried through the city streets.

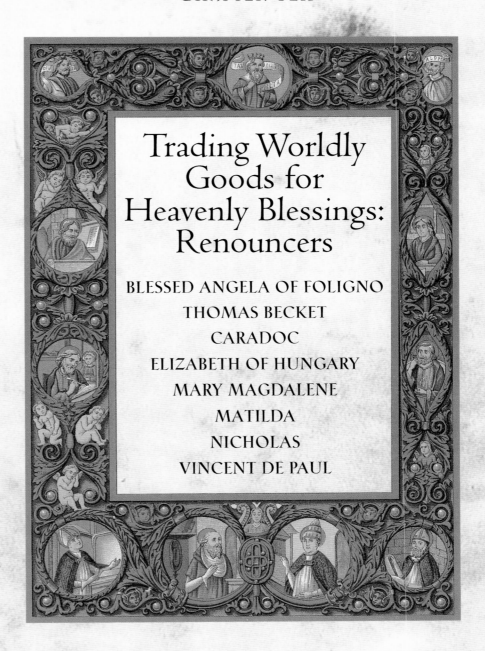

Chapter Ten

Trading Worldly Goods for Heavenly Blessings: Renouncers

BLESSED ANGELA OF FOLIGNO

THOMAS BECKET

CARADOC

ELIZABETH OF HUNGARY

MARY MAGDALENE

MATILDA

NICHOLAS

VINCENT DE PAUL

MANY SAINTS TURNED AWAY FROM THE MATERIAL WORLD IN ORDER TO BECOME CLOSER TO GOD. THIS IS ALL THE MORE NOTABLE AMONG THOSE WHO STARTED WITH GREAT WORLDLY WEALTH AND THEN RELINQUISHED THEIR MATERIAL GOODS TO CONCENTRATE ON SERVING GOD OR, LIKE ELIZABETH, USED THEIR RICHES TO MAKE OTHERS' LIVES RICHER.

BLESSED ANGELA OF FOLIGNO

JANUARY 4

Angela, born in Foligno, Italy, around 1248, to doting, well-off parents, married a rich man. A spoiled young wife and mother, she was utterly heedless of spiritual matters and, by her own account, not only pleasure-loving and self-indulgent but sinful. Nothing in her life foretold the sudden, radiant vision she received in her mid-thirties, of a redeeming path of penance and loving self-sacrifice.

Saint Francis was her example of joyful renunciation, and she became a tertiary of his order. For a time, Angela's external life did not change, but her ties to the world were gradually and painfully torn. First her beloved mother died, then her husband, and finally her sons. She suffered mightily, yet she shared Francis's faith in a divine, overarching wholeness that embraced joy as well as grief.

Her spiritual experience followed eighteen steps, encompassing rapturous ecstasies and profound humility. At the conclusion

PAGES 116 AND 117: Christ shattered the double standard when he defended Mary Magdalene. Her humble penitence for her worldly ways would inspire saints and others down the centuries. In Giovanni da Milano's fresco, she washes Christ's feet.

of her steps, she was subjected to years of agonizing temptations, first to the distorted manifestations of false humility, then to the cold, perverse bitterness of spiritual pride. Angela gathered a community of other tertiaries about her, many of whom gratefully told of being rescued from the brink of utter spiritual destruction through her. Today she is remembered as one of the great contemplatives, yet the charity and comfort that she bestowed was as earthly as her former worldly pleasures, and she brought to living a lightness of heart that was no longer carelessness but perfect surrender. Before she died in 1309, her final ecstasy was "an abyss of light—an abyss in which the truth of God was spread out like a road."

THOMAS BECKET

DECEMBER 29

Born in London in 1118, and raised and educated in a manner befitting his upper-class station, Thomas Becket enjoyed the pastimes and privileges of his time and continued to do so when, in his early twenties, he entered the service of the archbishop of Canterbury, who sent him to study canon law in Italy and France and, in 1154, made him archdeacon of Canterbury.

The following year, Thomas became royal chancellor to and the close friend of King Henry II, who employed the worldly cleric successfully in various political and military capacities. In 1162, Henry named Thomas archbishop of Canterbury, and immediately an astonishing transformation took place. The frivolous aristocrat, statesman, and soldier went from being, in his words, "a patron of play-actors and a follower of hounds, to being a shepherd of

The sacrilegious murder of Thomas Becket in a church, indeed, in Canterbury Cathedral itself, scandalized all Europe. Traditionally, churches were sanctuaries.

souls." He embraced a new austerity and turned his political genius to the protection of the poor and the Church.

His new spiritual course set him against his king, especially when Thomas claimed certain traditional royal rights for the Church, most notably the judging of the crimes of clerics. The archbishop was obliged to escape to France, and in his exile, away from the temptations of power, he was able to perfect his faith. Shortly after his return to England six years later, Thomas again fell afoul of his king.

Perhaps fulfilling their liege lord's wish, four knights beheaded Thomas Becket while he was at prayer in his Canterbury Cathedral in 1170. No sooner was his death made known than he was immediately and spontaneously recognized as a martyr throughout the Christian world. Three years later, Pope Alexander—who had not always supported Thomas in life—canonized the man the people had named a saint.

CARADOC
APRIL 14

As a harper at the court of South Wales, Caradoc held an enviable position in the world—until it took the fancy of the prince, Rhys ap Tewder, to hold the bard responsible for the death of two of the princely greyhounds. Having almost lost his life at a prince's whim, Caradoc had a sudden spiritual revelation of the emptiness of serving mortal rulers and turned to a divine Master instead.

Caradoc went to Llandaff, near Cardiff, there receiving the tonsure—the head-shaving that indicates admission to the clergy— of a monk from the bishop, who attached him to the church of Saint Teilo. From there, Caradoc went to Gower to live as a recluse, close to the abandoned church of Saint Cenydd. Later, he and a group of companions settled on a nearly deserted island in far western Wales, across from Pembroke.

The monks were driven from their solitude by raiding Norsemen, and Caradoc took charge of the monastery of Haroldston. In common with other hermits, he had a knack for commanding animals, rendering them tame and docile, as when he tamed a pack of hounds "by a gentle movement of his hand." He was greatly revered in his lifetime and was interred in Saint David's cathedral, in the parish of that name, with great honor, sorrow, and affection, when he died in 1124.

ELIZABETH OF HUNGARY

NOVEMBER 17

E lizabeth was a royal princess, born in Bratislava, the city of the Hungarian royal family (today in the Slovak Republic), to King Andrew II in 1207. From childhood, her story was one of piety lived gracefully, and her legend tells of a youthful melding of devotions and games.

At fourteen, Elizabeth was given in marriage to Ludwig IV, the ruler of Thuringia; the highborn husband and wife were very much in love and in spiritual accord. As a married woman in the public eye, Elizabeth continued her religious practices discreetly, loath to bring attention to herself. It is said that she had the long, elegant sleeves that were fashionable at the time fastened to her dresses only after she had heard Mass—although she dressed more modestly than the extremes of fashion dictated—and that she wore simple gowns in private. When she was fasting or eating only bread and water, she had herself served the same dishes as the others at the table but only pretended to eat.

The princess was especially given to the corporal works of mercy, tending the sick, giving food and drink to the poor and clothing them, preparing the dead and seeing to their burial. She spun wool for garments for the needy and sewed them herself. She is even said to have fished to feed them. In order to protect herself from the temptations of her high station, she took as her confessor and spiritual director Master Conrad, a man of rigorous ways, who on occasion had physical punishments inflicted on Elizabeth for the most innocent infractions of obedience.

Miracles abound in her story. In one case, beer kept flowing from a jug Elizabeth poured until all the thirsty poor were sated; when she finally looked, the pitcher was still filled to the brim. She founded a hospital at the foot of the mountain on which rose Wartburg Castle, her home; one day, as she rode to the castle with glass objects for the children of the poor wrapped in her mantle, the bundle fell onto the rocks below, but when her mantle was unfolded, everything was whole.

Elizabeth was energetic and joyful in everything she did, famous for weeping for Christ's suffering, but always with a radiant expression—her legend reports that her crying never made her ugly. Her husband, Ludwig, was deeply religious in his own right, admiring and supporting his wife's devotions, including periods of sexual abstinence—though the couple had three children—and endowing her charitable works. There is another tradition that holds that he was critical of Elizabeth's almsgiving; according to this legend, Ludwig once met his wife as she was taking an apronful of bread to the needy. When he asked to see what was in her apron, she opened it and a shower of roses tumbled out. (Roses are perhaps her most common attribute in art.) Ludwig's own religious bent inspired him to head off to the Crusades, but in 1227, Elizabeth's beloved husband of six years died suddenly in Otranto, Italy, before he ever set sail for the Holy Land. When Elizabeth heard of Ludwig's death, she went nearly mad with grief before turning once more to her spiritual source.

Tradition has it that Ludwig's brother, Heinrich

Bartolomé Esteban Murillo's lushly colored seventeenth-century painting of Elizabeth of Hungary emphasizes the humility of the saint—a queen physically caring for those afflicted with the most repellent diseases.

Raspe, immediately turned the princess and her three children out of Wartburg Castle, claiming it as his own. At last able to give herself to the poverty she had always treasured, Elizabeth refused her father's invitation to return home to the Hungarian royal court, instead taking the habit of the Franciscan third order and remaining in the world but practicing certain pieties. In her time, she was noted for having virtuously lived three of the conditions of woman—virgin, wife, widow—and is sometimes shown wearing a triple crown for that reason. From the day of her husband's death until her early death four years later in Marburg, Hesse, in what is today Germany. Elizabeth's life was one of prayer and care for the poor and the sick.

MARY MAGDALENE

JULY 22

Mary Magdalene was one of the women who prepared Christ's body for burial, and a jar of ointment is her emblem. Here, she holds the jar open, perhaps to recall the empty tomb of the Risen Christ.

According to Western tradition, Mary was a first-century young woman of wealth, position, and beauty, the daughter of Eucharia and Syrus, and the sister of Martha (p. 93) and Lazarus. The three siblings owned a great deal of property in and around Jerusalem, including the Galilean town of Magdala, but Lazarus was a soldier and Mary was such a slave to pleasure that Martha was left to take care of everything.

So spectacularly lost to virtue was Mary Magdalene that she was known only as "the sinner." But one day, in a moment of spiritual awakening, knowing that Christ was dining nearby, she ran to the place where he was with his disciples. At first she was too ashamed to go to him, but finally, the sincerity and relief of her penitence overcame her shame, and she knelt before him to wash his feet with her tears of love, then dried them with her long hair and soothed them with rich ointments. (Her emblem in art is a jar of ointment.) When those about him expressed their outrage at Jesus's allowing such a person near him, he chastised them for their lack of charity, giving Mary as an example of a sinner whose great love had earned her forgiveness.

There is a legend that Mary Magdalene was a disciple of Jesus, and that after his death, she preached and had disciples of her own. The gospels relate that she was one of Jesus's favorites—a paragon of the grace showered upon earnest repentance. Martha and Lazarus became followers of Christ as well, selling off all they had and giving everything to the apostles. Jesus loved Mary Magdalene so much that when Lazarus died, Jesus raised him from the dead; another time, Jesus cured Martha of a hemorrhage. Mary Magdalene was at the foot of the cross when Christ died, and she prepared his body for burial. She remained at the tomb when all the others had gone, so that she was the first to see the Risen Christ and received from him the mission to tell the others.

Her legend also tells that, set adrift with Martha and Lazarus, Mary Magdalene arrived with them at Marseilles, in the south of France, and after converting the whole city, lived in a holy cave for thirty years, never eating but living solely on the songs "of the heavenly hosts." When her time came, she called

for Maximinus, her traveling companion of long before, now a bishop. Her face was so radiant that Maximinus could scarcely look at her. He gave Mary Magdalene Holy Communion, and "her soul took its flight to the Lord."

MATILDA

MARCH 14

The daughter of Count Dietrich of Saxony and Reinhild of the Danish royal family, Matilda was born in Engern, Westphalia, around 895, and raised by her father's mother, an abbess. The young girl grew in loveliness and piety. When she was about fourteen years old, she married the son of the Duke of Saxony, Henry, some twenty years her senior, and known as "the Fowler" because he so enjoyed the aristocratic pastime of hawking. Their married life was harmonious and loving, a foundation of strength in a war-torn age, and they had five children.

Henry was elected king of Germany in 919, and ruled wisely, thanks largely to Matilda's counsel and prayers—as he and all their subjects acknowledged. Matilda was compassionate and openhanded, giving generously to those in need, often with her husband's support, and engaged in consistent religious devotions. Indeed, Matilda in some material ways lived almost as if she had taken orders, though with genuine humility she did not call attention to herself with external mortifications or sacrifices.

When King Henry died in 936, Matilda called for a Mass to be said for her husband's soul, then handed the priest the jewels off her body, as a sign that she was withdrawing from the public world. Her eldest son, Otto, was crowned king, though Matilda had favored a younger son, Henry (a third son, Bruno, was later canonized). Once on the throne, Otto began to criticize his mother for her donations to the Church and to the poor, even claiming that she was drawing on the royal treasury for her philanthropy. Sorrowfully, Matilda learned that Henry, too, had turned on her, and she ruefully remarked that though she was pleased that the quarreling brothers were now united, she could not help but wish that it were not at her expense.

The queen mother signed her inheritance over to her sons and left the court for the castle in which she had been born. The affairs of state began to deteriorate suddenly and alarmingly, and so con-vinced were the people that this was divine retribution for the king's treatment of Matilda that Otto, at the behest of his young queen, Edith, gave back all of Matilda's goods to her. Matilda returned to court and resumed her acts of charity.

Henry, too, ceased to torment his mother, but he did not desist from attempting to seize the throne, and in 955, Matilda prophesied his death. After the loss of Henry, Matilda spent the next decade establishing religious houses and traveling from one to the other. At Quedlinburg, Germany, in the year 968, the saint queen realized that she was dying and, according to her legend, began to give away everything in the sickroom around her. Finally, she was told that nothing remained except the linen that would make her shroud. One last time, Matilda prophesied: "Give that to Bishop William of Mainz"—her grandson—"he will need it first." And such proved to be the case. Matilda was buried next to her beloved husband and was venerated as a saint by the people of her realm from that moment on.

NICHOLAS

DECEMBER 6

Nicholas of Myra has been one of the best-loved saints in the calendar at least since the ninth century, when a highly colorful story of his life was first recounted in Byzantium; as early as the sixth century, there was a church in his honor in that city. During the fourth century Nicholas was bishop of the city of Myra, at the time one of the most important cities of the Roman province of Lycia. in what is today Turkey. In western Europe, he has been known since the eleventh century, when what were claimed to be his remains were taken from Myra to Bari, in southern Italy, perhaps to save them from the invading Turks. His relics are still enshrined there, and for this reason, he is sometimes called Saint Nicholas of Bari.

The only child of wealthy and pious Christian parents who lived together chastely after their son was born, the infant Nicholas was so holy, they say, that he nursed only once a day on Wednesdays and Fridays, the traditional fast days. As a young man, rather than pursue worldly pleasures with others of his age, he visited churches, learning by heart the Scriptures he heard read there. And when his parents died, leaving him very wealthy, he considered how to use his goods for the glory of God.

Living nearby was a wellborn man who had fallen upon hard times; this man had three daughters, whom he could not give in marriage because they had no dowries. The father had resolved that they should become prostitutes in order to support him. Nicholas learned of this and, determined to forestall this great sin, he secretly threw gold into the neighbor's house one night.

In the morning, the father found the gift, thanked God, and began to arrange his eldest daughter's marriage. The next night, Nicholas again threw his gift of gold into the neighbor's home, and this time the old man decided to discover who his benefactor was. Some days later, Nicholas again tossed gold in through the neighbor's window, and this time the old man chased Nicholas in order to thank him. He caught up with the generous young man, who made him promise to never tell the secret. For this reason, gifts are exchanged on the saint's day in some countries, and Nicholas is a patron saint of unmarried women. Saint Nicholas became known as Santa Claus in the United States through a Dutch form of his name, Sinte Klaas.

Nicholas is associated with the sea—he is the patron saint of sailors as well. One tale tells of mariners overtaken by a violent storm at sea. In desperation they prayed to Nicholas, who appeared and set to helping them with the rigging and sails. The storm abruptly stopped.

Many other miracles were attributed to the saint both before and after his death. As bishop, he was said to be "humble in his attitude towards others, persuasive in speech, forceful in counsel, and severe in his reprimands." When angels announced that his hour was at hand, Nicholas breathed his last with the words *in manus tuas*—"Into Thy hands (I commit my spirit)."

VINCENT DE PAUL

SEPTEMBER 27

Vincent, born around 1580, was the third of six children of Jean de Paul and Bertrande de Moras, farmers in southwest France, near the Basque country. Vincent was elected to receive an education on account of his lively intelligence

Lorenzo Veneziano's fourteenth-century painting portrays a blessing Nicholas holding the Bible—too sacred to touch with bare hands—recalling an early sign of his holiness.

and intellectual leanings; accordingly, he was sent to study with Franciscan Recollects, or Cordeliers, at the closest town and was ordained at the unusually young age of twenty.

In 1605, on his way back from Marseilles, Vincent was kidnapped by pirates and sold into slavery in Algeria; he escaped in 1607, and returned to France. From there, he went to Rome to continue his education and was sent from Italy back to France on a confidential mission to King Henry IV in 1609, the year before the king's murder. Vincent was strikingly handsome, and this may have contributed to his success at the relaxed court of Margaret of Valois, queen consort of Navarre, where he served as one of the worldly queen's chaplains. This preferment was in keeping with Vincent's life plan, which was to enjoy the greatest material comfort possible, but during this period there occurred one of several spiritual shifts that would move the young man toward sainthood.

Lodging with a friend in Paris, Vincent was accused of theft by him, but to all their friends, Vincent's simple, oft-repeated response was "God knows the truth." When, after six months, the real thief was discovered, Vincent spoke of this painful episode in conference with his spiritual directors, but as if it had occurred to someone else, so little did he wish to flaunt the humility with which he had endured his former friend's accusations.

Also in Paris, Vincent came under the guidance of a very holy priest, through whose agency Vincent came to know of the widespread spiritual deprivation of the peasantry, at times far more oppressive than their material wants. His mission, to bring Christians back to a wholesome practice, began in 1617, with the financial support of a pious couple, the Count and Countess de Joigny, in whose household Vincent lived as the countess's confessor. His successes were not only among the peasants, and later the convict galley-slaves of Paris and Bordeaux, but he also converted the Count de Rougemont and other licentious figures of the French aristocracy.

The Countess de Joigny and her husband endowed a community of missionaries to work among the country folk; Vincent became a member of the community upon the death of the countess. The members of this community, the Fathers of the Mission, are variously called Lazarists or Vincentians (the Society of Saint Vincent de Paul was founded some two hundred years later, in Vincent's honor). Today, the Vincentians still work primarily among the people of the countryside; in Vincent's lifetime alone, twenty-five houses were founded in Europe and as far away as Madagascar.

Vincent was tremendously active, a gifted organizer and fund-raiser once he overcame his lack of confidence. He raised vast sums from the wealthy nobility of France; some of the money went to ransom some twelve hundred Christian slaves in North Africa. In the controversies surrounding Jansenism—a reformist doctrine that maintained that free will was limited—Vincent was adamantly on the side of moral choice.

In all his actions, he maintained a remarkable calmness of mind, which derived from his continual openness to God. By nature, he was ill-tempered and quick to anger—in his own words, "hard and repellent, rough and crabbed." By grace, he was acutely sensitive to the material and spiritual needs of others. In his last years, Vincent was often very sick, and he died quietly in Paris on September 27, 1660. He is the patron saint of all charitable societies.

OPPOSITE: Vincent's open book symbolizes his mission to aid the common people. The fifteenth-century Portuguese artist Nuno Gonçalves emphasized the saint's compassion and physical beauty in this panel from the altarpiece in the saint's honor in the convent named for him.

Alphabetical Saints

Saint	Day
Agatha	February 5
Anastasia	December 25
Andrew	November 30
Anthony of Padua	June 13
Augustine	August 28
Barbara	December 4
Benedict of Nursia	July 11
Benedict of San Fredello	April 4
Bernadette	April 16
Blessed Angela of Foligno	January 4
Brigid of Kildare	February 1
Caradoc	April 14
Catherine of Alexandria	November 25
Catherine of Siena	April 29
Cecilia	November 22
Christopher	July 25
Clare of Assisi	August 11
Cosmas and Damian	September 26
Dominic	August 7
Dymphna	May 15
Elizabeth Ann Seton	January 4
Elizabeth of Hungary	November 17
Frances of Rome	March 9
Francis of Assisi	October 4
Francis Xavier	December 3

Saint	Day
Frumentius	October 27
Gemma Galgani	April 11
Geneviève	January 3
George	April 23
Gertrude of Helfta	November 16
Helena	August 18
Ignatius of Loyola	July 31
James the Greater	July 25
James the Less	May 3
Januarius	September 29
Jerome	September 30
Joan of Arc	May 30
John Bosco	January 31
John the Baptist	June 24
Jude	October 28
Juliana	February 16
Kateri Tekakwitha	July 14
Lawrence	August 10
Leo Karasuma	February 6
Lucy	December 13
Margaret	July 20
Martha	July 29
Mary Magdalene	July 22
Matilda	March 14
Michael the Archangel	September 29

Saint	Day
Monica	August 27
Nicholas	December 6
Patrick	March 17
Paul	June 29
Perpetua and Felicity	March 7
Peter	June 29
Reparta	October 8
Rita of Cascia	May 22
Roch	August 16
Rosalia	September 4
Rose of Lima	August 23
Scholastica	February 10
Sebastian	January 20
Sergius of Radonezh	September 25
Simeon the Stylite	January 5
Teresa of Avila	October 15
Theresa of Lisieux	October 1
Thomas	July 3
Thomas Becket	December 29
Ursula and the Eleven Thousand Virgins	October 21
Vincent de Paul	September 27
Vitus	June 15
Zita	April 27

Chronological Saints

Saint	Day
Geneviève	January 3
Blessed Angela of Foligno	January 4
Elizabeth Ann Seton	January 4
Simeon the Stylite	January 5
Sebastian	January 20
John Bosco	January 31
Brigid of Kildare	February 1
Agatha	February 5
Leo Karasuma	February 6
Scholastica	February 10
Juliana	February 16
Perpetua and Felicity	March 7
Frances of Rome	March 9
Matilda	March 14
Patrick	March 17
Benedict of San Fredello	April 4
Gemma Galgani	April 11
Caradoc	April 14
Bernadette	April 16
George	April 23
Zita	April 27
Catherine of Siena	April 29
James the Less	May 3
Dymphna	May 15
Rita of Cascia	May 22

Saint	Day
Joan of Arc	May 30
Anthony of Padua	June 13
Vitus	June 15
John the Baptist	June 24
Paul	June 29
Peter	June 29
Thomas	July 3
Benedict of Nursia	July 11
Kateri Tekakwitha	July 14
Margaret	July 20
Mary Magdalene	July 22
Christopher	July 25
James the Greater	July 25
Martha	July 29
Ignatius of Loyola	July 31
Dominic	August 7
Lawrence	August 10
Clare of Assisi	August 11
Roch	August 16
Helena	August 18
Rose of Lima	August 23
Monica	August 27
Augustine	August 28
Rosalia	September 4
Sergius of Radonezh	September 25

Saint	Day
Cosmas and Damian	September 26
Vincent de Paul	September 27
Januarius	September 29
Michael the Archangel	September 29
Jerome	September 30
Theresa of Lisieux	October 1
Francis of Assisi	October 4
Reparta	October 8
Teresa of Avila	October 15
Ursula and the Eleven Thousand Virgins	October 21
Frumentius	October 27
Jude	October 28
Gertrude of Helfta	November 16
Elizabeth of Hungary	November 17
Cecilia	November 22
Catherine of Alexandria	November 25
Andrew	November 30
Francis Xavier	December 3
Barbara	December 4
Nicholas	December 6
Lucy	December 13
Anastasia	December 25
Thomas Becket	December 29

Photo Credits

Index